me.plus

exploring the quest for
our true identity

David F Mansfield
Ruth E Filmer

ISBN: 9798496610636

I highly recommend this translation for all those who are serious about studying God's word.

All Greek & Hebrew word definitions from;

And;

Dedication

This book is dedicated to the memory of my father,

David John Mansfield,

Who was a glowing testimony to the power of God to change people's lives and restore their identity.

Miss you Dad.

In a world of growing confusion around human identity and where identity itself has become increasingly weaponised, it is important that we find some solid rock on which to stand and a trustworthy lens through which we can see. A Bible worldview champions the 'God-image' in humanity and declaring that 'in Christ' that identity is both recovered, redeemed and released. People want the freedom to choose who they are or who they want to be, but any consideration of who we are that excludes what God has both said and done will always deliver less than the 'very good' the Lord intended. In his book me.plus, Dave Mansfield encourages us to discover our God-shaped identity by rejecting the lure of autonomy and personal preference and embracing the model of our Maker.

Dr John Andrews, Bible Teacher and Author

I found the insights in this book fascinating, inspiring and revelatory. It has left me wanting to start, today, to find fullness in Christ with the clear and concise guide this book provides. It will be invaluable to Churches as they seek to find their true identity, collectively and individually. The easy to read and comprehend writing style of both its authors is wonderful. If a non-fiction book can be a page turner, this is it!

Hazel J Wilcox, Christian Author

In this excellent book, Dave, along with daughter Ruth, take us on a fascinating journey of discovery so that we, like Jesus, may function powerfully out of our true identity. Skilfully, the writers unpack the quandary of our confused, self centred, image and unfold how we can realise who we really are in Christ so we may live fruitfully from that revelation. And in that understanding, we are freed to successfully fulfil our God ordained destiny. This is essential reading. Easy to read with clear step by step teaching for the reader to absorb and apply for positive change, you'll find yourself unable to put "me.plus" down.

Barry Manson. Pastor, freelance speaker and author.

Contents

Introduction 9

Chapter 1: Preparing for change 13

Chapter 2: Valued...................................21

Chapter 3: Coming Home........................35

Chapter 4: Doing and Being......................43

Chapter 5: Living to Purpose......................57

Chapter 6: Becoming................................69

Chapter 7: Continuing 77

Chapter 8: Maturity 89

Chapter 9: Making It Work..........................95

Identity growth check-list...........................97

Appendix: The Technical Bit.......................99

Useful Scriptures....................................111

Further Reading 116

Other books by the same author 117

Introduction

Michelangelo is famous for saying that he worked to liberate the forms imprisoned in the marble. He saw his job as simply removing what was extraneous. This endless struggle of man to free himself from his physical constraints is a metaphor of the flesh burdening the soul.[1]

Michelangelo, hailed as the world's greatest sculptor, had a unique gift and a unique way of turning blocks of stone into great works of art. It is reputed [but hard to substantiate] that he said;

"I saw the angel in the marble and carved until I set him free."[2]

There is another version often found in some academic works;

"In every block of marble I see a statue as plain as though it stood before me, shaped and perfect in attitude and action. I have only to hew away the rough walls that imprison the lovely apparition to reveal it to the other eyes as mine see it."[3]

Many of us will identify with these thoughts. We feel like there is something more, perhaps even something spectacular, hiding within us. We need someone to take a chisel to our lives and set free the angel within the the stone. Michelangelo is also famous for a number of statues called, collectively, "The Prisoners". These largely incomplete works have men seemingly trying to break free from the rock - imprisoned by it. These are are first class images for the plight of mankind. We are created

---

[1] http://ahuskofmeaning.com/2011/08/michelangelo-at-the-accademia-part-2-the-unfinished-slaves/

[2] https://savedbydesign.wordpress.com/2019/04/04/i-saw-the-angel-in-the-marble-and-carved-until-i-set-him-free-michelangelo/

[3] https://www.michelangelo-gallery.com/michelangelo-quotes.aspx

individual, unique, for purpose, for success, but find ourselves trapped and struggling to break free.

Our desire is for significance. To be ourselves and make our own mark on the world. To be what we were created to be, to do what we were created to do. To feel like we belong. To understand who we are. To break free from the stone that holds us.

Understanding who we are is foundational to the way we do and experience life. As Christians, our life is in Christ, and our sense of identity should flow from there. This book will address the issues of personal identity, self worth, self awareness, the true nature of freedom to be ourselves, and what it means to be in Christ. Our understanding of these issues will determine how we live our lives and serve our God. This is not about "feel-good", it is more about purpose. Although, understanding identity and purpose will inevitably make us feel better! For a clinical definition of identity see the appendix.

This book is born out of a module I was asked to teach on identity. As I researched the subject I found myself inspired and wanting to provide something more than a teaching module. The objective is to provide some answers to what are, very often, un-asked questions. So many struggle with confusion about identity and purpose, low self esteem and a sense of being lost in this world. For others it is a nagging insecurity and lack of confidence.

Over the following pages, it is my hope that you will discover who you are in Christ - your true identity, and that you are valued and built for purpose. That the church is your home and a safe place to grow, that you can be confident in the Spirit of God within you, and that discipleship is your friend and not your enemy.

One of the great joys for me in this project is the inclusion of two guest chapters written by my eldest [and entirely brilliant] daughter, Ruth. She brings with her some great insights and, with her background in psychology and church leadership, displays a gentle wisdom that will enrich you as you read this book.

Ruth has written one of the chapters and consulted on others. She has also provided a very useful appendix.

The book is a journey. It is written out of a number of convictions;

1. Our sense of identity shapes our lives

2. Our sense of identity can be reshaped!

3. There are things that "science" has to teach us

4. There are greater things that the Bible has to teach us

5. That the Church is our home

6. That discipleship is our friend

7. That we can become the people we were created to be

A strong sense of identity is;

Consistent

- A state of being that is "us" in any environment

- Recognisable [measurable]

- We have some understanding of it

- People who know us recognise it

Predictable

- Knowing who we are means that we can predict our responses and how we will be in various circumstances

Core

• It is the very centre of us

• Shapes our lives and our attitudes

• Forms our expectations

• Determines how we feel about ourselves and life

Therefore, identity is of vital importance.

What will get us through this life with a genuine sense of achievement? What will enable us to feel fulfilled? What will make us fruitful and productive? What will make us secure in relationships? What will make us secure in our relationship with God?

Finding the real you and being secure in your identity.

Being the person God designed, created and calls you to be.

I pray that, through this book, you will come to a place where you will allow the great sculptor to chip away at all that holds you back, and release you from the stone into all that He has for you.

There is a teaching programme that goes with this book, we would be happy to deliver that for you and your church. There are contact details at the back of the book.

Chapter 1: Preparing for change

The problem is me!

*Someone once said, "constant change is here to stay"!
For growth, change is necessary and inevitable. Nobody
really likes change, the more we can ready ourselves for
it the better.*

*This chapter seeks to challenge preconceived positions
that might stop us from embracing the new, and
becoming all we can be.*

> *Identity; ...who a person is, or the qualities of a person
> or group that make them different from others.[4]*

And therein hangs the problem. I don't know who I am,
what sets me apart.

So much in life finds fruitfulness and resolution in our sense
of identity. Our sense of self will either enhance or
undermine our opportunities to feel fulfilled, successful,
loved, accepted, competent, valued, significant and more.

Our sense of identity will manifest in confidence or
insecurity. It will effect our outlook on life and our
engagement with it, our relationships, and our faith.

Our modern culture continually draws us to examine
ourselves, be dissatisfied, invest in some product, system
or ideology that will fix us, and leaves us, usually, in a
worse state.[5] We find ourselves on a treadmill of trying to
become something we were never created, or expected,
to be. In our desire for significance, we often miss the
obvious and plough ourselves indiscriminately into

---

4 Cambridge English Dictionary

5 For further discussion on culture see the appendix.

whatever is served up to us by the media and other influencers.

We seek out others who share our feelings of inadequacy, who manifest the same traits. We find some comfort in the thought that we are not alone in our perceived flaws. The "group identity" keeps us safe. We succumb to the voices that seem to speak with authority, and allow our lives to be shaped into something which we learn to become comfortable in, but never fulfilled.

We crave acceptance. We want to feel loved and liked. We want others to value and respect us.

Our sense of self is compounded by what we think we see in the mirror, the things people say to us and about us, attitudes shown towards us, formal feedback and critiques.

For some, we overcompensate, feeling the need to profess how brilliant and attractive we are. We talk ourselves into believing that we are capable of anything. We are invincible, nothing can touch us. Then when we are, inevitably, touched, it all falls apart.

Even those of us who find faith, after the honeymoon period, when the real work begins, are faced with trying to work out where we fit, what our role is, what is our contribution?

All in all, finding the real me is not an easy job, and I am prone to complain about it rather than do anything about it. I'll go with the flow because its easier. Social media is filled with complaints, disillusionment, sadness and unfulfilled expectations, but not many people doing anything positive about it. We have become professional complainers who are content to just put it out there and leave it.

But the drive to discover the real me doesn't disappear that easily. It shouldn't. My sense of identity, who I believe I am, will determine how I think, what I do, what I say, the relationships I form, the career I pursue, the focus of my life.

The problem with me is... me, the way I see myself and, consequently believe others see me. It is an unavoidable foundation upon which my life is built. If it is shaky, then I will never feel that things are really alright, never be sure I'm doing the right thing.

Many seem to feel that identity is a static, unchanging thing. This is not true. There are elements which will not change but in other areas our sense of identity can and will change as we engage with the process of development. My self-perception can change when I find success in something, get a promotion, win a competition, fail an exam, wreck a relationship. All of these things can impact on our sense of self. If we approach life the right way, we can become something different, see ourselves differently, and be happier about it!

The journey starts with discovering who I am right now and building from there.

Discovering who we are could change our world. The question is where and how should we seek out this identity, looking in the wrong place can damage us, listening to the wrong voices will lead us astray.

But don't worry, help is at hand!

> Gen. 1:26 Then God said, "Let us make man in our image, after our likeness.

Whatever your theological view of the early chapters of Genesis, the inescapable truth that we are presented with is that we are God's idea. His design and creation. Your mission, should you decide to accept it, is to take the journey that leads you to understand that design and live in your true identity.

We carry the image of God

We are designed to reflect Him, His personality, His attributes. If you think about all of the good things we know about God, those things should find some reflection in our lives.

Living in our true identity, in this reflection, will help us to become fruitful, fulfilled, connected, secure and happy. That is not to say that we will no longer experience hard times, but our sense of self will provide the resources for us to manage the difficult times and come through to the fulness of life Jesus intends for us.

This works because we are tapping into God's design, the way He created us. We, as we pursue His plan, will become what He created us to be, do what He created us to do, and see Jesus glorified in us. This is our true identity, our purpose.

We all carry this image, but we may need to dig deep to find it. For many, it has been buried under years of taking on board false information, distorted because of the things we have thought, said or done, lost because we have failed to nurture it.

John Maxwell uses the word "actualisation" to describe the happy position of becoming the fulness of the real you [for further definition see appendix]. Actualisation comes as a work of the Holy Spirit. As we pursue Jesus, the Spirit will mould us into His likeness and draw out that image of God in us. But we have to give the Spirit something to work with. The following chapters will provide a road map to that actualisation. To find our true identity, the person God designed and made us to be, to discover our connection to each other, and to realise our uniqueness in this Universe and in the plan of God.

As we reflect on this, we are challenged by three elements at work within us, these elements sit at the core of our being.

1. The Image of God
    That reflection of God that exists in every human being as we have observed over the last few paragraphs.

2. Inner Formation
    The way we have been shaped by the life we have lived. The way we were brought up, the impact of influential people, relatives, teachers, leaders, friends, colleagues, heroes, villains, pretty much anyone who has left any kind of imprint on our lives. The books we have read, the films we have watched, the things we love, the things we hate, the things we believe. All of these things will have shaped the person we are and our view on life, the Universe, and everything else. Once established, these elements continually reinforce our sense of self and any faulty thinking can be hard to shift.

3. Sin Distortion
    The image of God, and the truth that has helped form the good in our lives, is distorted by the power of sin. Our view of what is good and righteous is distorted by our rebellion against God, that's what sin is! We deceive ourselves that our position is right, is good, is logical and sensible. This only serves to build and compound our sense of guilt, shame, and worthlessness. We experience these things primarily in our insecurity and general sense of being lost.

So, we are a mixture of what God created us to be, what life has formed in us, and what sin has distorted in us. To discover our true identity, we have to make that journey back to the Image of God. But we have some rivers to cross to get there!

First challenge; be prepared for change

There are many online jokes and memes regarding change. We don't like change happening around us and we don't like change in ourselves. We have become comfortable with who we are, even though we don't like ourselves! Because of this, we have formed a life view, and we react badly, defensively, to anything that challenges that view.

Your first challenge is; are you going to allow some new information to change your life view?

There is a dynamic know as "Confirmation Bias".

> *Confirmation bias occurs from the direct influence of desire on beliefs. When people would like a certain idea or concept to be true, they end up believing it to be true. They are motivated by wishful thinking. This error leads the individual to stop gathering information when the evidence gathered so far confirms the views or prejudices one would like to be true.*

> *Once we have formed a view, we embrace information that confirms that view while ignoring, or rejecting, information that casts doubt on it. Confirmation bias suggests that we don't perceive circumstances objectively. We pick out those bits of data that make us feel good because they confirm our prejudices. Thus, we may become prisoners of our assumptions.*[6]

Why is it important to understand this? Because we all hold views that have no real substance other than, perhaps, a single experience that has created a feeling. We translate that feeling into a "truth". That is how we become prisoners of our assumptions. The information we gather either supports our position or we reject it. When

---

[6] Shahram Heshmat, Ph.D., associate professor emeritus at the University of Illinois at Springfield.

we feel we have gathered sufficient information to support our position, it becomes our "truth". We, essentially, believe lies about ourselves. We don't believe something good could happen to us, that we could become something bigger, better. This is a challenge we will need to overcome by receiving and accepting some new information.

For example, I am going to make the case, later in this book, that discovering the real you can only really be achieved when you are properly engaged with the church.

Some of you will already be having a negative reaction!

Maybe, in your past, you didn't get what you wanted or needed from a church. Maybe you were offended by something the minister said or did. You got hurt. In the pain of the experience, you have formed a view of the church. Every time you hear some criticism of the church it adds fuel to your fire - you don't stop to check the facts or ask if you are having a reasonable reaction, you simply let your dislike of the church grow. This is Confirmation Bias. We take information that agrees with our feelings to be true, without investigation, and dismiss the rest.

Other commentators have called it "My-side Bias". Their point is that we get good at seeing the flaws in opposing arguments but are consistently accepting of anything that reinforces our own view - usually without any kind of verification. If it suits our bias, we will accept anything, even though it might cause us harm.

This dynamic will sink any chance we have of growth and discovery.

We must approach our quest for a new sense of identity, not naively or open to anything, but with an openness to properly consider and evaluate the call of God and His image in our lives, understanding that it is our current bias that has got us in to the state we are in.

As my friend, Pastor Phil Curtis, observes; *"When a believer exercises faith in one area, it effects their faith in other area's. In the same way, when a believer tolerates sin in one area, it causes them to justify sin in other areas."*

Our complaint needs to be put on hold whilst we consider a way forward. We need to consider the things that we have allowed to form our inner person. We need to acknowledge and receive forgiveness for our sin and learn to live better lives. And, having done these things, chart a path to the new me, the true me, the me that God created me to be. We need to find consistency in doing the right things in order that our inner person will be reshaped into the likeness of Jesus.

I'm told that it only takes 63 days to form a habit [see appendix]. This happens as we consistently do something. This technique is often used by sports coaches, breaking down the target into manageable pieces and making habits of those pieces. But we do need to see the big picture so that we know what we are aiming at.

So, prepare yourself. Its time to adjust your paradigms, get a fresh view, work on the right things and allow your God-given identity to form and rise up.

What now?

- Reflect on your life to date, ask the questions;
  - I am stuck in a rut where my thinking is concerned?
  - Do I hold attitudes or ideas having no real idea where they came from?
  - Am I ready to receive, validate and properly respond to new information?

Chapter 2: Valued

Believing the right things

We all hold beliefs. The trouble is, we're not always sure where they came from. This chapter seeks to challenge us in coming to a place of right belief so that we have a sure foundation to work from.

Foundational for understanding and developing our identity is to come to a place of faith about the things that God says about us. I say "come to a place of faith" because reading and understanding the words doesn't necessarily mean we believe the words! If we don't believe the words then they won't affect us. You can tell what a person believes by the way they live their lives. Our lives should be found firmly rooted in Christ and the truths that the scriptures speak over us.

I have always held that faith is largely a decision. I decide to believe what God says and choose to live in it - living like I believe it. This in itself is a challenge. But more than that, we need to ask the Holy Spirit to give us revelation [divine, supernatural understanding] of the truth.

God says "You are pretty fantastic!" Believe it!

Of course our self-image and our outlook have been distorted by sin. All those things which we say, think or do that offend God, have an impact on our lives. Our sin causes death to our inner person and brings distortion to our perception. Most of us have trouble believing the truth about ourselves because of this. We think it egotistical, illogical, unlikely, it must be nonsense. But if God says it, it must be true! We have been spoilt by sin, that is a fact. But, of course, God supplies the solution in the cross. And the cross provides two very important things for us, justification and sanctification.

Justification and Sanctification

Roms 3:23 ...for all have sinned and fall short of the glory of God, 24 and are justified by his grace as a gift, through the redemption that is in Christ Jesus, 25 whom God put forward as a propitiation by his blood, to be received by faith.

When you put your faith in Jesus, you receive justification as a grace gift. That is to say, you haven't earned it, and you don't deserve it but, because He loves you, God has given you this gift. This gift is provided through the blood [the sacrifice on the cross] of Jesus. So what does justification do for us? Well, because of the cross, our sin counts no more - its just as if I'd never sinned! My slate is wiped, and remains clean and clear of all sin, past, present and future. All is covered by the cross. Yes, I still sin, I need to deal with that, but when I mess up I shouldn't beat myself up over it. I should repent [decide to live differently], receive forgiveness, and return immediately in my head and heart, to my justified state - which didn't actually change through any of this process because God's forgiveness is unwavering.

Because of this justification, I no longer need to carry the weight of my sin, Jesus has taken that. Communication with the Father is now re-established and the work of sanctification begins.

1Cor. 6:11 ...But you were washed, you were sanctified, you were justified in the name of the Lord Jesus Christ and by the Spirit of our God.

Sanctification means being made, or becoming, holy. Both justification and sanctification can be understood as an event; the cross did all that was necessary in that moment when Jesus died for our sin. Sanctification, though, is also a process.

Hebrews 10:14 For by a single offering he has perfected for all time those who are being sanctified.

We were sanctified by the work of the cross and, day by day, as a work of the Holy Spirit in the power of the cross, we are being sanctified. In other words, the Holy Spirit is continually at work in us, transforming us, bit by bit, into the likeness of Jesus. We need to co-operate with this work, part of this work is the renewing of our minds, giving us a proper perspective and restoring the image of God in us.

One of the powerful effects of this work is that it should be the end of guilt and shame. I say should be because, again, this is something we need to believe and, in a sense, appropriate for ourselves. As we engage with the process, the cleansing of justification and sanctification should bring us to a place of real freedom. Freedom from guilt, shame, fear and anything else that prevents us from entering into the reality of what God made us to be. Imagine never feeling guilty again, free from any condemnation. What a glorious thought. The truth is that, if you have put your faith in Jesus, that is who you are!

Take a moment to let that settle in.

I am who you say I am

If we don't engage with these realities, we can become hesitant in approaching God because we are not sure if, as sinners, we will be welcome and accepted in His presence. But this is actually what the work of the cross is all about.

If I understand, and believe, that my sin is paid for, that I am being changed from the inside out, that God created me to be spectacular, things start to change.

Being in Christ breaks the chains. We are set free to be the person we were designed and created to be. We no longer face condemnation from the Father. The Spirit of life now works in us to bring us to maturity. Mistakes are quickly and easily dealt with. Life takes on new meaning. We have a battle in our minds that we need to win in order to get to this place. Elephants in captivity, when they are young, have their leg tied to a piece of wood to stop them running away. They become so conditioned by this that, when they are big and strong, they could, if they wanted, break free. But in their minds this little piece of rope cannot be overcome. We face a challenge here if we are to find freedom. We remove the old conditioning by replacing it with something better, this will require a journey in our thinking.

In his letter to the Romans, the Apostle Paul spends seven chapters explaining the process of sin and destruction, the plight of man and the work of the cross. Then, in chapter 8, we reach this incredible climax, a proclamation of the great work God has done; we are now free!

> *Rom. 8:1 There is therefore now no condemnation for those who are in Christ Jesus. 2 For the law of the Spirit of life has set you free in Christ Jesus from the law of sin and death.*

He shares a similar sentiment in 2 Corinthians;

> *2Cor. 5:17 Therefore, if anyone is in Christ, he is a new creation. The old has passed away; behold, the new has come.*

The net result of the work of the cross is that, for those who believe, there is a new birth. The old me is consigned to that great big black hole where God puts things that He has decided to forget. The old has passed away. The new has come. We must now decide to live in the new.

Tim Keller says;

Like Paul, we can say, 'I don't care what you think. I don't even care what I think. I only care about what the Lord thinks.' And he has said, 'Therefore, there is now no condemnation for those who are in Christ Jesus', and 'You are my beloved child in whom I am well pleased'. Live out of that.

Believer, you are a new creation, free now to live up to the design of the maker, free to be the real you, free to be spectacular!

We now face the challenge of living in new norms and living differently. We have a new book in which to write our life story.

Establishing new norms is a big part of the challenge. If we are to successfully live in our real identity, the past must be consigned to death so that the new can live.

Our new normal is that we are free. Free from guilt and shame because of the cross. Free to enter into the Father's presence. Free to live a new life and become all that He created us to be.

Our constant challenge is that our new normal is challenged by the old and the World culture[7] around us. That is why the Apostle Paul makes the point that the past is gone; the old has passed away. We must let it go. Let it die. Let it pass away. We must not allow the past to interfere with the present.

If we tolerate the interference of the past, the new is too easily corrupted. Old habits undermine the new ones. The old me tries to drag me back. This is where faith really kicks in. I must believe what God says. I am who He says I am. I am no longer the old me, I am a new creation and must live like one, forming new habits and living a new lifestyle.

---

[7] For further discussion on culture see the appendix.

Mind and Spirit

Understanding and living in our new, true identity, must start with understanding and revelation about our value. If we don't believe God values us then we won't take God seriously. If we don't believe we have value then we won't take ourselves seriously. With no sense of value our lives become devoid of purpose and meaning. Ultimately, in our own eyes, we become worthless. This feeling of worthlessness is at the root of much of our depression and insecurity. We don't treat ourselves with respect because nobody else treats us that way.

A recent article at unheard.com covered the following;

> *British schoolchildren are having an existential crisis? You might have missed it, but a huge global survey by the OECD of 15 year-olds across 79 countries was published last week [2019], in which UK young people placed second-to-last in the world in what they call the 'meaning in life index'.*
>
> *That's right, of all the teenagers on the planet, ours are among the least likely to agree with the idea that "my life has clear meaning or purpose".*
>
> *And yet, this unsettling news was pretty much ignored. The focus in the media was on the survey's news about 'modest improvements' in reading and maths. The meaning of life stuff was left well alone.*
>
> *The same survey suggested that the UK's young people, while being in the middle of the pack in terms of happiness, also rank near the very bottom in terms of life satisfaction. Of all the countries surveyed, only the children of Turkey and the Macao region of China rate their life less highly than the British do.*

These feelings of hopelessness and worthlessness are not restricted to our teenagers. Many of us reading this will be feeling the same. It is so common now that we don't even talk about it.

We can overcome these feelings if we have a better developed view of our personal value. That development must take place in our mind and in our spirit.

Understanding what God says about us is key, but it is one thing to read the words, another to understand, and yet another to have revelation.

Revelation occurs at the point the information sinks into our spirit, through the help of the Holy Spirit, and becomes real to us.

It is no longer simply information, it is now transformation through truth.

Both mind and spirit are required to engage in this.

The Image of God

> *Gen. 1:26 Then God said, "Let us make man in our image, after our likeness. And let them have dominion over the fish of the sea and over the birds of the heavens and over the livestock and over all the earth and over every creeping thing that creeps on the earth."*

> *Gen. 1:27 So God created man in his own image, in the image of God he created him; male and female he created them.*

What does it mean to be made in God's image?

> *The creation of humankind is set apart from the previous acts of creation by a series of subtle contrasts with the earlier accounts of God's acts.[8]*

---

8 Expositor's Bible Commentary (Revised). General editors: Tremper Longman III and David E. Garland. Published by Zondervan. Grand Rapids, Michigan 49530, U.S.A.

Then God said, "Let us make man in our image"
God's word that follows the standard "Let there be" is
superseded by "Let us make."

"after our likeness"

Every other creature is made "according to its own kind".
The creation of humankind specifically notes that the man
and the woman were not made "according to their own
kind." They were made "in [God's] image". They are not
just like each other, they are also like God; they share a
likeness to their Creator.

"male and female he created them"

This creation is specified as "male and female". Gender
has not been highlighted in this account of the creation of
the other forms of life, but for human beings it is clearly
very important. The narrative puts great emphasis on the
fact that God created man as "male and female."

"let them have dominion"

Only human beings have been given dominion in God's
creation. Humankind's dominion is clearly stated to be over
all other living creatures: those of the sky, sea, and land.

How are we separate from the rest of creation?

• A different perspective and intent in the creative process

• A different responsibility

• A different culture

How are we like God?

• Reflecting His character and nature

• Here to achieve His purposes

Where is this image?

For most, it is buried under a lifestyle of sin!

Whilst sin in itself has been dealt with at the cross, it still effects our lives if we continue in it. Our sense of self gets bent out of shape.

The mirror that reflects God in us is covered in dust and muck. Occasionally, something might sneak out, and we catch a glimpse of the reflection.

Wonderfully Made

Humankind is singled out from the rest of creation, and for some fairly significant reasons.

The creation process is beautifully described for us in Psalm 139.

> *Psa. 139:13 For you formed my inward parts; you knitted me together in my mother's womb. 14 I praise you, for I am fearfully and wonderfully made. Wonderful are your works; my soul knows it very well. 15 My frame was not hidden from you, when I was being made in secret, intricately woven in the depths of the earth. 16 Your eyes saw my unformed substance; in your book were written, every one of them, the days that were formed for me, when as yet there was none of them.*

"formed my inward parts"

Inward parts; *kilyāh, used 31 times in the OT; kidney; by extension: inmost being: heart, mind, spirit, the seat of thought and emotion of the inner person; kernel (of wheat).*[9]

God designed and constructed our thinking and emotions, all of the stuff that makes me who I am.

---

9 Kohlenberger/Mounce Concise Hebrew-Aramaic Dictionary of the Old Testament, John R. Kohlenberger III, Editor, William D. Mounce, Editor, Copyright © 2012 by William D. Mounce.

Seeing this as a seed helps us to understand that there should be growth and that whilst God has formed us, this is only a starting point.

"Knitted me together"

suḵ, used 10x in OT; to anoint, to use oils or perfumes or lotions; to put on lotions; to be poured on; this can refer to the application of oils, perfumes, lotions, or resins to the body. Also; to hedge about, fence in.

This section carries the idea that God gathered all of the important elements of who we are and mixed them perfectly together.

The idea of oils carries images of anointing and worship.

"Fearfully and wonderfully"

yārēʾ, used 317x in the OT; to revere, respect; to be awesome... in other contexts fear relates to honour, respect and awe, as in "the fear of the LORD".]

You are awesome!

This awesomeness should cause us to honour and respect God!

"Known"

"My frame was not hidden from you, when I was being made in secret", "Your eyes saw my unformed substance..."

God knew you before anybody else did.

He monitored your development and growth. He watched His plan coming together!

"Planned"

"...in your book were written, every one of them, the days that were formed for me, when as yet there was none of them."

In God's world there are no accidents! If a child is conceived it is the plan of God. A plan which existed before conception and became reality at conception. Your life was designed and sanctioned by God before you came to be.

In order for us to be secure in our identity, we need the assurance that our creator God loves us and is here, helping us.

Unconditional love

Unconditional love is a phrase which is used regularly by Christians, though it doesn't always mean what most people want it to mean.

> *John 3:16 "For God so loved the world, that he gave his only Son, that whoever believes in him should not perish but have eternal life. 17 For God did not send his Son into the world to condemn the world, but in order that the world might be saved through him."*

The experience of God's love and grace come to us through the sacrifice of Jesus. The cross of Jesus is all about restoration of relationship with God so that we can experience His love. Salvation is the means by which this is achieved. Salvation is received through faith, not by being or doing good, which may in itself be admirable, but will not save us as we will still fall short of God's standards.

The purpose of eternal life is that we live as we were designed and purposed to live, in the intimate presence [love] of God, forever.

Such is God's love for you;

> *Rom. 5:6 Christ arrives right on time to make this happen. He didn't, and doesn't, wait for us to get ready. He presented himself for this sacrificial death when we were far too weak and rebellious to do anything to get ourselves ready. And even if we hadn't been so weak, we wouldn't have known what to do anyway.* [The Message Version]

This is the measure of God's desire for your well-being. That He does not wait for you to come to your senses, but sends Jesus to set the record straight and give us the opportunity to know Him and receive all of the goodness He has prepared for us.

Because He values you. And because the God of the Universe values you, you are truly valuable. And loved.

And, did I mention that you are awesome?

Meditation

Simply understanding this is not really enough. In order for these truths to properly shape our inner person, we need to make sure that they become a part of us.

Meditation, pondering and reflecting, on these issues, will help us.

I am not talking about the sort of meditation where you sit and empty your mind, but the sort where you actively fill your mind with truth from the Scriptures and begin to express it.

> *Joshua 1:8 This Book of the Law shall not depart from your mouth, but you shall **meditate** on it day and night,*

so that you may be careful to do according to all that is written in it.

The Hebrew word for *"meditate"* used here is;

hāgāh

> *This means "to utter a sound, moan, meditate; to mutter; from the base meaning of uttering a sound of any kind comes figure of meditation, the act of thoughtful deliberation with the implication of speaking to oneself.* [10]

I am told that the priests used to form the habit of *"mumbling"* the scriptures to themselves as they walked along in order to be sure the word of God was taking root in them.

Learning and repeating the scriptures will help, speaking them out will be even better. There are many ways of doing this.

The Navigators produce some great materials for learning and remembering Bible verses.

You could just make a list of helpful verses and keep them in the front of your Bible, as you pick it up each day to read, you could review the verses and sit and ponder them.

You could write out some verses and stick them around the house, put one on the mirror, one by the kettle, anywhere you regularly stand still for a moment.

Treat the word of God as food for your spirit, and make sure you have a good meal every day!

---

[10] Kohlenberger/Mounce Concise Hebrew-Aramaic Dictionary of the Old Testament (KM Hebrew Dictionary), John R. Kohlenberger III, Editor, William D. Mounce, Editor.
Copyright © 2012 by William D. Mounce

What now?

- Reflect on your understanding of your value;
  - Do you know you are valued by God?
  - Do you know you are valued by others?
- Generate a strategy for assimilating this so that it is not just information;
  - Talk to someone
  - Read the scriptures
  - Pray, ask God to help

Chapter 3: Coming Home

No man is an island entire of itself; every man is a piece of the continent...[11]

We were not created for isolation. Our true home is found in relationship. Relationship with God and with His church.

This chapter seeks to encourage meaningful connection with the fellowship of believers; the church.

If our identity is a flower, the church is the soil and the Holy Spirit is the water. Both are necessary for us to become all we are created to be. A flower will not thrive if it is separated from this environment.

Identity and connectivity

In this chapter we are going to talk about the church.

"But what has that to do with my sense of identity" you might ask?

The church is God's plan for our personal growth and development. The church, actually, is God's plan for most things! Community answers many of questions that we are presented with as we endeavour to understand our identity and mature in it. God did not design or create us to fly solo, relationship is key to growth and maturity.

You were created to be part of the church! You cannot find the real you without it.

We will use Paul's letter to the Ephesians as our template here, though there are many other passages we could use if we wanted to.

---

[11] From MEDITATION XVII, Devotions upon Emergent Occasions, John Donne

The Body

Eph. 1:22 And he put all things under his [Jesus'] feet and gave him as head over all things to the church, 23 which is his body, the fullness of him who fills all in all.

Paul refers to the church as "the body" nine times in this letter.

This body, over which He [Jesus] is the head, is His fulness!

So, in these verses, we see these thoughts...

• Jesus as supreme ruler [all things under His feet]

• Is given to the church [as supreme ruler]

• Which is His body

• Filled with Him!

Everything that can be experienced of Jesus in this life can be experienced in the church.

Whilst some things might be experienced in other environments, the church is the place where His "fulness" is experienced.

Fulness: *plērōma, that which fills up; full measure, entire content.*

Everything!

Church is the place that God has provided for you to discover who you are and become who you are intended to be.

You are called here to live in His fulness so that you can be filled. This is far more than just the church being His hands and feet. This is far more than just family.

True identity can only be found when you connect with the fulness of Christ, found only in the church.

Eph. 2:4 But God, being rich in mercy, because of the great love with which he loved us, 5 even when we were dead in our trespasses, made us alive together with Christ—by grace you have been saved— 6 and raised us up with him and seated us with him in the heavenly places in Christ Jesus, 7 so that in the coming ages he might show the immeasurable riches of his grace in kindness toward us in Christ Jesus.

Notice, with the backdrop of Paul's comments about the church, how he continues to speak in the plural. There is no concept in the New Testament of doing Christianity on your own. Being a Christian is being part of the church. We need each other and will not see God's plans or purposes achieved without each other.

Real life in Christ; alive together with Christ

We participated in Christ's resurrection from the dead, and it means we too live now. Though our physical resurrection awaits the end of the age, again Paul has brought eschatology into the present. What will happen physically has already happened spiritually, since we are "in Christ." Formerly "dead," we now live. Formerly dominated by the power centre of the world system, we now live through the power of the Holy Spirit.[12]

Seated in heavenly places

Raised us up with him means that, because of Christ's resurrection, those who believe in him are given new life spiritually in this age (regeneration).[13]

There is more to come in the next life, but this life is continuously interrupted by signs of new life and position because we have been raised up with Him.

----

[12] Expositor's Bible Commentary

[13] Wayne Grudem, ESV Study Notes

In Christ

Whilst our physical resurrection with Christ is yet to come, each follower of Jesus enjoys presently the benefits of being "in Christ".

We are made alive in Him, raised up with Him, seated with Him. And whilst this might not be a fully physical realisation yet, the benefits are very real. This reality brings communion, life, and an authority to live that life. We are alive, raised and seated with Christ. "In Christ" is a permanent and unbreakable arrangement, He is ours and we are His forever. This should be cause for great confidence and, of course, celebration.

When God raised Christ from the dead and seated him in the heavenly realms, he raised and seated those "in Christ Jesus" with Him. What happened to Him, happened to us. We have a seat in the Kingdom of God which carries a wealth and authority for this life, and the promise of an incredible future.

All found in His church!

Discovering the riches of God's grace, finding relationship with Him, is foundational to understanding identity, and is found in the church.

The gift ministries of Ephesians 4

> *Eph. 4:12 ...to equip the saints for the work of ministry, for building up the body of Christ...*

The gift ministries of Ephesians 4 are given to the church, for the church, to equip and build us up.

Building up [*oikodomē*] has to do with strengthening, advancement and edification. It has to do with building solid foundations.

Sitting under these ministries should, in practice, help the internal building process of soul and spirit which give form to our God given identity. This should happen in the church.

Love

> Eph. 4:2 ...with all humility and gentleness, with patience, bearing with one another in love...

The church is, or at least it should be, a place of love!

Filled with the love of Christ, filled with the love of His people for one another.

This is the place for encouragement!

> Eph. 4:15 Rather, speaking the truth in love, we are to grow up in every way into him who is the head, into Christ, 16 from whom the whole body, joined and held together by every joint with which it is equipped, when each part is working properly, makes the body grow so that it builds itself up in love.

Love permeates everything.

Church is the place for honesty; being honest and receiving honesty. Speaking truth to one another in love! Make sure you registered that; *"in love"*.

The flow of love through the ministries of the church should make it a safe place to be vulnerable and open for some inner shaping and growth.

The Church as a place of accountability

Accountability is one of the essentials for growth and identity development.

Accountability is necessary for progress.

The foundation of love in the church makes correction without judgement possible.

We, for our own sakes, need someone in our lives who gets to say "no" to us when necessary.

> Eph 5:21 ...submitting to one another out of reverence for Christ.

As part of a list of things constituting good behaviour, Paul challenges us to mutual submission - in other words; we allow others to speak into our lives and we listen to what they have to say!

This is one way of showing our reverence [respect] for Christ.

This is also essential to development.

We are family

> Eph 2:19 So then you are no longer strangers and aliens, but you are fellow citizens with the saints and members of the household of God, 20 built on the foundation of the apostles and prophets, Christ Jesus himself being the cornerstone, 21 in whom the whole structure, being joined together, grows into a holy temple in the Lord. 22 In him you also are being built together into a dwelling place for God by the Spirit.

In context this passage is talking about Jews and Gentiles. As Gentiles, we find ourselves invited and fully accepted into this family that God is building.

No longer strangers; because we have been joined together by God as His church.

Christ being the cornerstone; the foundation and key to success, "*joined together*", thoroughly linked into one another.

Growing into a Holy Temple; through fellowship and discipleship, to become a dwelling place for God!

TO BECOME A DWELLING PLACE FOR GOD!

Me and the church

Jesus said;

> *Matt 28:19 "Go therefore and make disciples of all nations, baptising them in the name of the Father and of the Son and of the Holy Spirit, 20 teaching them to observe all that I have commanded you. And behold, I am with you always, to the end of the age."*

The great commission requires the making of disciples. The process of discipleship is the responsibility of the church. This process is what transforms us.

The journey of being and doing that shapes our inner person to look more and more like Jesus takes place in the context of fellowship where we must be accountable and proactive.

The church is God's plan. It's His plan to save the world. It is also His plan to transform lives. The context for this transformation is fellowship and the work of the Holy Spirit.

The proper development of our identity can only be successfully done through a work of the Holy Spirit in fellowship with the church.

Choose carefully

Of course, all churches are not the same.

For your own safety, growth and journey to maturity, you need to choose your church carefully, and then stay there!

Church hopping will not help you. If you move churches every time you're not happy with something you will never grow. If you move every time you disagree, it will not help you. If you move every time you receive correction or direction, you will not mature.

Make sure you ask questions of a church before joining!

How do you view fellowship? How do you process mentoring and discipleship? How do you handle correction? What are your pathways for growth and opportunities to serve?

These questions would be good starting places.

Pray, ask God where He wants you to be. Join and then stick with it!

Setting down proper roots in a church family is essential to discovering your identity and growing in it.

What now?

- Reflect on your feelings about church;
  - Do you feel at home?
  - Are you growing?
- Read Paul's letter to the Ephesians in one sitting
- Talk to your Pastor1

Chapter 4: Doing and Being

I have heard it said that being is more important than doing. A thought that puts the two things at odds with each other. This is a false dichotomy. This chapter seeks to restore the balance of being and doing in such a way that it promotes growth in our sense of identity.

Do-be-do-be-do

It is said that there is a graffiti in the Guggenheim Gallery, New York, that says;

> *To do is to be - Plato*
> *To be is to do - Aristotle*
> *Do be do be do - Frank Sinatra*

Strangers in the night, a famous Frank Sinatra recording, is reputed to have the first recorded incidence of extemporaneous singing. Whilst recording the vocal, Sinatra, clearly at home with himself and the studio, began singing freely along to the melody; "do-be-do-be-do".

I have heard many messages, read many books and articles, that want us to believe that "to be" is more important than "to do". I believe this does not give us a balanced view.

Firstly, let's separate value from significance [being and doing].

We are valued because of the way God feels about us [see chapter 3].

> *Jer. 31:3 I have loved you with an everlasting love; therefore I have continued my faithfulness to you.*

Value has been given to us since before the beginning of time. Before any of our days came to be, the God who designed and created us, planned a life for us and celebrates His creation, places value on us way beyond anything we could imagine. Our value is found in Him and Him alone.

Our significance is found in the balance of being AND doing. These two things, whilst seemingly opposites, are intrinsically linked.

What we do is born out of who we are [our being]. Who we are is shaped by what we [consistently] do.

Our being is shaped by revelation [understanding] and by what we do. Understanding we are God's creation, knowing He has a plan for us. Knowing that He has given us all we need to become and to do all He created us for.

There is a saying that is found on many social media platforms;

God doesn't call the equipped, he equips the called!

This is a false dichotomy, and shows a limited understanding about the way God has worked! God designed and created you for purpose, for significance. His design is perfect. You were born with the attributes God wants you to have in order to serve Him the way He wants you to. You were equipped before you were born. You were born already called and equipped.

> *Ephesians 2:10 For we are his workmanship, created in Christ Jesus for good works, which God prepared beforehand, that we should walk in them.*

Your task now is to discover what that purpose [call] is, what call and equipping you were born with, and engage in the good works God has prepared for you.

Over the course of my life, as I write I am 64 years old, I have invested in a number of personality profiles designed to highlight who I am, my strengths and my weaknesses. This profiling was done over a period of nearly 30 years. I accessed different types of profiling; Myers Briggs, SIMA, Strengths-finder and others. What is interesting is this, that each system, even though they were very different in the way they assessed me, provided many of the same excellent insights into who I am and what my strengths are. There were some additional bits of insight which varied, but the core attributes of who I am were consistent and unchanging. I possess a core set of gifts and abilities which have served me my entire life in whatever situation God has placed me in. The key here is to allow God to do the placing!

The revealing of these gifts and strengths help me with my sense of identity. I still, though, have to learn to engage with these gifts, refine them, and follow God's leading in order that my sense of identity will be shaped to God's design and no-one else's. This is where "doing" plays a part.

For the Christian, the primary route to inner change is discipleship. What we do!

The purpose of discipleship is that, through disciplined **doing**, we become better **beings**. My inner person is reshaped by the Holy Spirit as I consistently do the right things. Our doing gives the Holy Spirit something to work with.

Random doing creates "being conflict". Undisciplined doing [being blown about by every wind] will cause confusion and conflict in the inner person. This conflict can lead to mental illness, even breakdown. There is an acknowledged disorder known as *cognitive dissonance*, it refers to the stress and discomfort caused when you think one thing but do something different [see appendix for further development of this]. This can cause all sorts of inner conflict and lead to feelings of disappointment and depression. Our doing, if we are to grow and establish a right sense of identity, must be properly ordered and follow Biblical principles.

What we do and who we do it with will have enormous impact on both our sense of identity and well-being. You will notice I have now added something to the equation; context. Being and doing require an appropriate environment to grow and develop.

Jocelyne Cesari of the Berkley Centre, makes the following observation about radicalisation;

> ...it is important to bear in mind that religion is not only belief, but also belonging and behaving. That is why de-radicalisation programs that focus on changing beliefs are usually not successful. Most radical groups do not focus on belief but rather tend to accentuate the belonging and behaving dimensions of religion.

Here, in another context, we see this principle at work. What we do, and the environment we do it in has great impact on our being. We are shaped by the disciplines and the environment, but we need to choose carefully and be sure that we are radicalised by love.

Our sense of belonging to our church family will give rise to new behaviours through the church's culture and discipleship and faith grows as a result.

We all carry paradigms. A paradigm is, essentially, a world view, the lens we look through as we observe what goes on around us. I remember, many years ago, listening to John Wimber talk on this subject in relation to the Holy Spirit and healing. What we believe [being] accompanied by experience [doing] and environment [church], will determine how well we minister to people. Biblical discipleship is the primary agent in shifting our paradigms. The imitation of Jesus is the best solution to the "me" problem.

Our doing should transform our being to such an extent that our doing, now flowing from our being, becomes much more natural. Our environment should provide a safe place for this to happen.

disciplined doing > enhanced being > natural doing

I will not be secure in my sense of identity if what I do is at odds with who I think I am. The primary point of change here is to work on what I do.

This is how discipleship should work.

Jesus' disciples became who they were called to be through a programme of watching, learning and doing, consistently - day after day, so that, over a three year period, ministry became instinctive because the inner person had changed, had been reshaped by the discipleship.

The programme [discipleship] and the environment [being with Jesus] enabled inner change that empowered ministry to flow more naturally from the inner person.

The Imitation of Jesus

When I was a young Christian, I used to hear people say, "I want to be like Jesus". I don't hear that so much these days.

Our objective, as Christians is to be transformed into the likeness of Jesus.

> *2Cor. 3:18 And we all, with unveiled face, beholding the glory of the Lord, are being transformed into the same image from one degree of glory to another. For this comes from the Lord who is the Spirit.*

We, those who love and follow Jesus, get to gaze on His beauty [worship], and as we gaze we are set on the journey of being transformed into His likeness - we reflect His glory. How does that happen? Clearly there is a work of the Spirit here, but there is also the challenge of discipleship; adopting His lifestyle.

The Holy Spirit has the power to just change us overnight. I remember clearly when I came to faith. Overnight my language cleaned up and my desire for drink disappeared. I could not have done that - certainly not overnight. It was a work of the Holy Spirit, a sign that something had changed because He had now filled my life. But there were still things that needed to change, things I needed to work on.

My aim is to become transformed into the image of Jesus, that is to say, I'm still me but there is an overwhelming family resemblance! Achieving that requires a three pronged attack;

• The ongoing work of the Holy Spirit

• Disciplined living following God's instructions

• Connecting and engaging with the right people and the right environment

This "doing" will shape our "being" and we will discover our true identity

The work of the Spirit

I don't know about you but, predictive text is both a joy and stressor for me. I have often sent texts that do not say what I want them to say because my phone has put words in I did not mean to say.

Predictive text works from your history. Your device learns, from past messages, the sort of things you say in your messages. It then predicts what you want to say in todays messages. Sometimes it gets it gloriously right, sometimes I find myself sending a second message because the first one was wrong thanks to this software that is supposed to save us time.

Life is a little like that.

We need the Holy Spirit to be our predictor and not allow our past life to interfere. As we embark on this journey, our past will want to reclaim some of our new life, get us back into the old habits. In order to fight against the old life and live in the new, we will need the help of the Holy Spirit. And that is alright because that is one of the reasons He was sent to us.

Finding the balance

We must be careful where we choose to place emphasis and ensure that our journey has as much balance as possible.

For instance, an over emphasis on doing can too easily devalue life. If we can no longer "do" we can become disposable, life can cease to have value if we cannot perform. That path leads us to end results such as adopting euthanasia for those we feel have outlived their "usefulness".

People can easily be seen as assets and then valued on their ability to be fruitful. These issues of identity are not our principal source of value, God is!

The point of discipleship is to reinforce your being through doing the right things, and not to create a false value system where we are only valued for what we do.

People who are more concerned about "being" are prone to selfishness and do not engage well with purpose. This lack of balance would seek to rob us of the important and necessary expressions of our faith which we are all called to. "How I feel" becomes more important than "what should I do".

Living as Jesus lived should draw out the true nature of who we are, His creation, bearing His image, continuing His mission, and help us to find the balance of being and doing. That is the nature of discipleship and the first steps to understanding who we are.

A word about grace

Position and Performance

When God looks at us, He looks at us in terms of our position; free, forgiven, cleansed, seated with Christ! We tend to look at ourselves in terms of performance; how well am I doing, am I good enough?

We need to discover God's grace and learn to see ourselves as He sees us!

For many, the idea of discipleship is quite irksome. We don't like people telling us what to do. We don't like rules and regulations. We prefer grace!

The problem is that most of us don't really understand grace.

What is grace all about?

The good news is that the grace of God has provided a solution for our rebellion. Because of the work of the cross, the sacrifice of Jesus, our sins are forgiven. Whatever debt to God our sins produced has been paid in full at Calvary. Thank you Jesus!

This means that, because of my faith in Jesus, my eternal future is secure, no matter what happens now.

The confusion comes in understanding the difference between punishment and consequences.

Is. 53:5 But he was pierced for our transgressions; he was crushed for our iniquities; upon him was the chastisement that brought us peace, and with his wounds we are healed.

Punishment for sin was dealt with at the cross. The "chastisement" [punishment/severe reprimand] that brought peace and reconciliation with God, for you and I, was put on Him. Punishment is no longer an issue.

Psalm 103:10 He does not deal with us according to our sins, nor repay us according to our iniquities.

Consequences, however, still exist! I will reap what I sow. And, whilst it is true that God, in His grace, sometimes removes the consequences, mostly He doesn't. If you sow love, you reap love. If you sow hatred, guess what?

If we sow the right things into our lives, our being is enhanced by our doing. Subsequently, our doing flows more naturally from our being.

Our confidence for this new understanding of self is provoked by the understanding of what God has to say about my value and my purpose. Working that understanding into my sense of identity requires discipleship. It requires a properly programmed journey, overseen and assisted by someone who is at least a little further along the journey. It will inevitably mean someone, hopefully someone we have learned to trust, helping us to understand what we should do, and holding us to account.

To live in the full experience of grace requires a committed walk of discipleship. Being and doing.

The nature of Discipleship

As we read through the Gospels, there are five observable strands to the Jesus method of discipling His followers. These are the primary elements we need to engage with to mature in faith and be sure of our identity.

Prayer

> *Luke 11:1 Now Jesus was praying in a certain place, and when he finished, one of his disciples said to him, "Lord, teach us to pray, as John taught his disciples."*

Jesus taught His disciples to pray. Prayer is the lifeblood of the Christian, it is about relationship, communication with God. It is as much about listening as it is talking, hearing what God wants to say to you. It is a two way street, a conversation not a shopping list. It feeds inner development.

The "Lord's" prayer [Luke 11] is an excellent example, it starts with relationship, worship and intent. It addresses God with the intimacy of Father. It provokes worship; hallowed be your name! It confesses a desire for the will and purposes of God; Your [not my] kingdom come, Your [not my] will be done. It petitions for provision, it clears the decks [forgive us, as we forgive]. It calls for help in times of temptation.

We must learn to pray.

Preaching

Jesus taught them to preach, and commissioned them to do it! Jesus starts His own ministry with a proclamation;

> *Luke 4:18 "The Spirit of the Lord is upon me, because he has anointed me to proclaim good news to the poor. He has sent me to proclaim liberty to the captives and recovering of sight to the blind, to set at liberty those who are oppressed, 19 to proclaim the year of the Lord's favour."*

He then went out and fulfilled this manifesto by preaching, teaching, healing and working miracles. He called His disciples to do the same.

In Matthew 28, He commands His disciples to make more disciples [that's us] teaching them [us] to do everything He [Jesus] taught them!

Every Christian is a missionary. Our mission field might be across the world or across the street, but it is part of our calling. The ability to use our words to share our faith and make a proclamation of the Gospel is essential. There is an interesting dynamic that takes place when we do this; our confidence in God grows! Our confidence in who we are in Him grows!

Pastoral

Mark 6:7 And he called the twelve and began to send them out two by two, and gave them authority over the unclean spirits. ...12 So they went out and proclaimed that people should repent. 13 And they cast out many demons and anointed with oil many who were sick and healed them.

Pastoral work is the work of caring. Praying for the sick, visiting those in trouble, providing for those in need, all are hallmarks of the Gospel and are evident in the life of Jesus. People need encouragement. It is our role to provide it. The ministry of healing is also part of our privilege package and essential if we are to imitate Jesus.

Perspective

He teaches them to be smart.

Matt. 16:11 "How is it that you fail to understand that I did not speak about bread? Beware of the leaven of the Pharisees and Sadducees." 12 Then they understood that he did not tell them to beware of the leaven of bread, but of the teaching of the Pharisees and Sadducees."

Don't be fooled by the culture of this world[14], it is predicated on a lie! Jesus taught His disciples to be smart. To identify the truth and distinguish it from a lie. To respond in a Godly manner. To handle the scriptures correctly.

Power

> Luke 24:49 "And behold, I am sending the promise of my Father upon you. But stay in the city until you are clothed with power from on high."

It is impossible to follow this path without the help of the Holy Spirit. His indwelling power is what will get us through, keep us on the straight and narrow. His power will change us and equip us. It is He who has the power to bring change, healing, deliverance.

These five things formed the backbone of the Jesus discipleship training programme, we too should learn to engage with all of these things if we wish to become like Him. As we engage we will begin to see more of the real us - that which Jesus created us to be and proclaims over our lives.

The disciplined doing of following the Jesus discipleship method, with help from the Holy Spirit, will reshape our inner person so that our being, our sense of identity, grows stronger and more and more into the image of God.

Discipleship is good for you!

---

[14] For further discussion on culture see the appendix.

What now?

- Do you feel you have found a good balance between doing and being?
  - If not, how will you address this?
- How open are you to the work of the Holy Spirit?
  - Invite Him to play a greater role in your life
- Are you properly engaged in a discipleship journey?
  - If not, talk to your Pastor

Chapter 5: Living to Purpose

A strong sense of purpose will guide us through life and draw the best out of us. Being "in Christ" is foundational here. This chapter seeks to instil the essential sense of God's purpose in all of us.

The truth about who we are is found essentially in what God says about us. Understanding the care and precision God has devoted to us and our lives will provide a different perspective and a foundation for living.

Our friends, family, work colleagues, teachers, leaders, idols, heroes, politicians, sometimes it feels like the whole world, wants to tell us who we are and who we should be. We are beset with conflicting information. We have unreasonable expectations placed on us. We too easily come to believe the wrong things about ourselves.

The story is told of a young man, many years ago, driving along in his Model T Ford. The car broke down and the young man, being a mechanic, set about fixing it. He tried everything he knew but, alas, could not get the car to go. After a while, an old man drove by in a limousine. He pulled over and after observing for a few minutes, spoke to the young man and suggested an adjustment to a specific part of the engine. The young man thought "What could this old guy know about this car that I don't?", but he decided he would give it a try. Having made the adjustment the car engine sprang back to life. The young man turned to the old man and asked, in disbelief, "How did you know that?" The old man replied, "My name is Henry Ford, I invented this car!"

You would expect that the inventor [creator] would know everything about his invention. That he would probably be the best person to talk to if something is not working. If we have questions about our lives, who we are, why we are here, should we not be consulting the creator?

Here are a few things the Bible tells us on this subject which we can use as a starting point.

Predestined, according to the purpose, before the beginning of time...

To understand the nature of our God given identity, Psalm 139 will again be helpful as it describes both the attitude and intent of God alongside the heart cry of the Psalmist. We will examine it in sections.

In this Psalm, David turns to God for vindication in the face of critical enemies. He invites God to examine him. It is in this context that we find some excellent data concerning the way God works in creation, specifically the creation of His children.

> *Psa. 139:1 O Lord, you have searched me and known me! 2 You know when I sit down and when I rise up; you discern my thoughts from afar. 3 You search out my path and my lying down and are acquainted with all my ways. 4 Even before a word is on my tongue, behold, O Lord, you know it altogether. 5 You hem me in, behind and before, and lay your hand upon me.*

God knows His children.

The Psalmist reflects on the closeness and intimacy of the God who "knows" him. The Lord is not just a casual observer of his life, but follows every detail. He knows David intimately, knows who he is, knows what to expect from him, knows what he is going to do or say next! David has been searched and known, and confidently asks God to examine him and make a judgement on his integrity.

God knows his thoughts, God persists in watching over him. The presence of God completely surrounds him.

It is only God who can do this! He knows us intimately. His presence surrounds us. Regardless of what is going on, He loves us and watches over us.

> *Psa. 139:7 Where shall I go from your Spirit? Or where shall I flee from your presence? 8 If I ascend to heaven, you are there! If I make my bed in Sheol, you are there! 9 If I take the wings of the morning and dwell in the uttermost parts of the sea, 10 even there your hand shall lead me, and your right hand shall hold me. 11 If I say, "Surely the darkness shall cover me, and the light about me be night," 12 even the darkness is not dark to you; the night is bright as the day, for darkness is as light with you.*

The inescapable Father

Wherever you are, God is there! Its the nature of being God [omnipresence], but is purposeful when it comes to His children - in life and death, day and night - there is no escape from the Father.

But why would you want to? His presence is not impotent, He is here to lead and guide, holding us in all situations, lighting the way, straightening out the path, giving us vision and revelation.

The omniscient God

This passage is a reminder that this is God; all knowing; beyond our comprehension.

He knows us, and knowing us, chooses us and remains with us! Our sense of identity should begin to flow from this knowledge.

The Psalm then takes a strange turn, David continues;

> *Psa. 139:19 Oh that you would slay the wicked, O God! O men of blood, depart from me! 20 They speak against you with malicious intent; your enemies take your name in*

vain. 21 Do I not hate those who hate you, O Lord? And do I not loathe those who rise up against you? 22 I hate them with complete hatred; I count them my enemies.

David's prayer here is less slandering, destroying the reputation of the wicked, as contrasting his view and feelings against theirs. He is wanting to show that there are two clear ends to this spectrum; the place were he stands and the place where the wicked stand. He is wanting God to recognise his full commitment and worship as opposed to the attitudes of the wicked. He has worked hard to live a Godly life. He hates who God hates! He cannot stand those who are against the Living God. This hyperbole is designed to show total commitment to God and His purposes.

Psa. 139:23 Search me, O God, and know my heart! Try me and know my thoughts! 24 And see if there be any grievous way in me, and lead me in the way everlasting!

Having asserted his devotion, David invites his God to inspect his motives to be sure they are pure. David is responding to accusations from men, but takes his plea to God! To battle with men leads to destruction, to turn to God for vindication leads to life, fellowship and growth.

The truths set out in this Psalm tell us a great deal about ourselves.

God had a plan for you before you were born, He formed/moulded you according to His plan. You are fearfully and wonderfully made according to His purpose.

Let that settle in you.

Formed according to His plan and purpose. Made for significance. Uniquely designed to make a difference. There is no-one like you, you are designed and created for something specific and, whilst clearly there is some growing and preparation to be done, you have all you need to become that person. Your sense of identity should be affirmed from this knowledge.

Understanding this is cause for worship. Understanding this should give you security and confidence; God has built you for the life He's called you to! If you are pursuing that life, you are ready, you are equipped, you are empowered. Because you are being you. The real you!

> *Phil. 3:7 But whatever gain I had, I counted as loss for the sake of Christ. 8 Indeed, I count everything as loss because of the surpassing worth of knowing Christ Jesus my Lord. For his sake I have suffered the loss of all things and count them as rubbish, in order that I may gain Christ 9 and be found in him, not having a righteousness of my own that comes from the law, but that which comes through faith in Christ, the righteousness from God that depends on faith— 10 that I may know him and the power of his resurrection, and may share his sufferings, becoming like him in his death, 11 that by any means possible I may attain the resurrection from the dead.*

What does it mean to be in Him?

Being found in Christ refers to the saving relationship we have with Him. We are saved and have relationship by virtue of putting our Holy Spirit inspired faith in Him. This salvation, and for Paul the glorious relationship that cannot be separated from our salvation, is his reason for living. This is his entire life focus.

This relationship is where he discovers who he is!

The status afforded him by the trappings of the world, and for Paul the accolades were many, are worthless to him because he only finds himself, and hence real life, in his relationship with Christ. Our challenge is to remove ourselves from the culture and practice that served to separate us from God and surrender our lives to Him. Having done so we find ourselves and our freedom!

Part of the problem is our inherent desire for "things", this can keep us from God. Paul counts the accolades of the world as rubbish. In his "worldly" life, he used some of the gifts God gave him to elevate himself and pursue a quasi-religious agenda. He also used the ways of the world and its culture to achieve the plaudits of his peers. It seems clear that Paul wanted to pursue what he thought were the purposes of God, but somehow got lost in the culture of the religious world he lived in. Then he met Jesus and it all changed. The culture of the world[15] promotes the following unGodly virtues;

Selfishness

The foundation of sin is that we put ourselves first; usually at the expense of others. For a being created to serve God to turn and serve self is the height of rebellion. Rebellion, of itself, separates. Relationship is broken. Our sense of identity is distorted.

Greed

The world culture continually feeds our desire for more. More money than we need, more food than we can eat, more status than we deserve, more power than is good for us. Greed always wants bigger and better. Greed consumes us eventually with a need for things we cannot attain. This need becomes the focus of our lives, all else disappears over time. Our sense of identity is distorted.

Pride

I have been to a number of funerals where the grieving relatives wanted Frank Sinatra's "I did it my way" played for the committal. They wanted people to know that the deceased had lived life on his own terms, had not been

---

[15] For further discussion on culture see the appendix.

subject or submitted to anyone or anything. One cannot underestimate the power of grief, but I wonder how many people stop to think about where the deceased is now? Pride removes God from any life equation. It proclaims that God is insignificant, that we have made it on our own! Pride puts us on the pedestal where Jesus belongs. Our sense of identity is distorted.

The renunciation of God

The accumulated effect of these traits, imposed on us by world culture, is the renunciation of God. In 1966, the New York Times printed a headline stating *"God is Dead!"*, you might imagine the shock waves! The reality is that, just a few years earlier, they would not have dared to print such a headline. For many it was an outrage. But for others, it confirmed something they had thought, or even believed, for sometime. World culture, whilst it wants to be seen to be tolerant of faith groups, wants to deny the existence of God. The created denying the creator is a recipe for disaster. How do you fill the gap that is left? With hedonism; living to please yourself and do things that you think will make you happy and fulfilled! This is the world we live in. Our sense of identity is distorted.

What is the nature of this rehabilitating faith?

If we put our faith in Jesus, we abandon the culture and philosophy of the world. Armed with Holy Spirit revelation, we understand that the trappings of this world are essentially worthless. Any kind of status or heritage is rendered meaningless in light of the cross. Money and power have no real value. For Paul, even his zealous religiosity was worth nothing. All that counts is a new creation! The only really valuable thing in life is knowing Jesus. All else flows from there. A fresh start with a clean slate. Our sense of identity gets restored.

When we put our faith in Jesus, we are made new, set free, given a fresh start. It is from this place that we can truly discover who we are and find our place in the world - in relationship with Him.

> Rom. 6:11 So you also must consider yourselves dead to sin and alive to God in Christ Jesus. 23 For the wages of sin is death, but the free gift of God is eternal life in Christ Jesus our Lord.

Sin is death to identity. Sin, actually, is death to everything! Jesus provides the solution!

> Eph. 1:3 Blessed be the God and Father of our Lord Jesus Christ, who has blessed us in Christ with every spiritual blessing in the heavenly places, 4 even as he chose us in him before the foundation of the world, that we should be holy and blameless before him. In love 5 he predestined us for adoption to himself as sons through Jesus Christ, according to the purpose of his will, 6 to the praise of his glorious grace, with which he has blessed us in the Beloved. 7 In him we have redemption through his blood, the forgiveness of our trespasses, according to the riches of his grace, 8 which he lavished upon us, in all wisdom and insight 9 making known to us the mystery of his will, according to his purpose, which he set forth in Christ 10 as a plan for the fullness of time, to unite all things in him, things in heaven and things on earth.

A word about predestination

Predestination can be a confusing topic for many. The idea that some hold to is that everything in life is fixed, or predestined. Many blame the theologian Calvin for this view, although I don't think this is what Calvin was driving at. Some think that everything is a matter of choice, many blame Arminius for this view, although I don't think this is what he was driving at either. In this passage the word "predestined" is used twice, so it is important that we understand what is going on here.

The Greek word, *proorizo*, is used six times in the New Testament. It means; to limit or mark out beforehand; to design definitely beforehand, ordain beforehand.

So, it is clear that there is a pre-existing plan in place that will, because God is the planner, come to fruition. But what is "predestined", and what isn't?

In the context of Ephesians, we should note that Paul speaks in the plural. That is to say that, he is talking about the church and not individuals. Is it predestined that you would become a member of the church? It would be hard to justify that idea. But there are things which are clearly predestined for those who do become, through faith, part of the church. Those who are in *"the chosen one"*, Jesus, are predestined to be adopted, redeemed, forgiven, saved and receive an inheritance.

These things are the plan of God, which existed before the beginning of time, and will happen because that is what is decreed [*predestined*] for the church.

This is not the same as *"foreknowledge"*. Foreknowledge is what God knows about you in advance because He knows you intimately [ref Psalm 139]. Because of the depth to which God knows you and His omniscience [knowing and understanding], He knows what you will do or say next, what choices you will make, which direction you will take. Foreknowledge is not the same as predestination, knowing something will happen [foreknowledge] is not the same as prescribing it [pre-destination].

With that understood we can now make sense of this passage.

Eph. 1:3 Blessed be the God and Father of our Lord Jesus Christ, who has blessed us in Christ with every spiritual blessing in the heavenly places, even as he chose us in him before the foundation of the world, that we should be holy and blameless before him.

God chooses [picks out and invites] us in Christ. Christ is chosen before the foundation of the Earth to be Saviour and Lord. Because we are now in Him, we benefit from that choice. Because we are in Him we are blessed with every spiritual blessing. The result of that choice is that the church stands holy and blameless before Him.

God sees you now in Christ, and no other way! God sees you as Holy [*set apart for Him*]. God sees you as blameless; as if you had never sinned!

In love he predestined us for adoption to himself as sons through Jesus Christ, according to the purpose of his will, to the praise of his glorious grace, with which he has blessed us in the Beloved.

Having been [through our faith response] separated out into the church, the predestined plan of God swings in to effect. We are adopted as sons. Sons have rights and privileges. Sons have an inheritance. Sons have responsibilities. Sons, by the way, includes the daughters here! The language of sons is used because, in its cultural context, sons typically benefitted far more than daughters. Paul is wanting us to understand that as "*sons*" we inherit everything.

According to His purpose means we are saved from something for something. God saves us from the pit we have dug for ourselves in order that we might engage with the purposes He created us for. God has a plan which He will fulfil, we are part of this plan and our lives carry purpose according to His grace which we experience through Jesus. If you remove Jesus from the equation, everything collapses.

Eph 1:7 In him we have redemption through his blood, the forgiveness of our trespasses, according to the riches of his grace, which he lavished upon us, in all wisdom and insight making known to us the mystery of his will, according to his purpose, which he set forth in Christ as a plan for the fullness of time, to unite all things in him, things in heaven and things on earth.

We are redeemed, the price of our freedom is paid. We are forgiven. All of our thoughts, words and deeds that are offensive to God, past, present and future, are forgiven because of the blood of Jesus.

We are given insights into His will and purpose. He calls us to be part of the plan. But, its hard to be part of the plan if you don't know His plan for you!

We understand that all things come from and lead back to Christ [including us!] He IS the centre.

How does this all help us?

We were designed and created for a purpose. There is, at the core of us, the finger-print of God. Our life, if we believe, is now in Christ.

Therefore we are free! Free to be ourselves - free to serve Jesus.

We are called! There is a role that only you can fulfil! You are not an accident, whether your parents planned you or not, God planned you before the beginning of time!

We have purpose! The things we were designed for are the things prepared in advance in order for us to use our gifts, abilities, insights, attitudes, passion and energy.

All of this is found in Christ!

If we are in Christ, all of this is ours!

This is who we are!

Our best identity can only be found In Christ!

What now?

- Are you living with a sense of purpose?
  - Can you identify consistent strengths and abilities in yourself?
  - Are you presented with opportunities to use those abilities?
  - If not, talk...
    - To your friends
    - To your Pastor
- Do you feel free?

Chapter 6: Becoming

Developing a strong sense of identity is not achieved overnight. It takes a journey, and intent. We can, with help from the Holy Spirit, reshape our inner self, we just need to make the journey. This chapter seeks to lay some foundations for ongoing development.

The ongoing nature of identity discovery and development

The identifying and developing of our identity, and understanding of it, is a lifelong process. The good news is that it gets easier.

The foundations are built first.

When this is established, it is down to fine tuning.

After time we should understand ourselves well, but we can still surprise ourselves.

The fine tuning never stops.

Journey

We shouldn't feel under pressure to achieve this all at once! This is a journey of discovery and development.

The important factors for sustained growth are belonging, behaving and believing.

Belonging; our environment is important, get settled in the right church.

Behaving; finding consistency in "doing" that positively shapes our "being".

Believing; the right things about God and about ourselves.

Continuity of doing and being

Consistency is our friend! We need to be focussed on consistently doing the right things. This can take time!

Random doing creates "being conflict".

Undisciplined doing [being blown about by every wind] will cause confusion and similar conflict in the inner person.

This conflict can lead to stress, mental illness, even breakdown.

Balance is important. An overemphasis on doing can too easily devalue life. As we have observed before, if we can no longer "do" we become disposable. Life ceases to have value if we cannot perform. This can lead to faulty values such as euthanasia. People can become assets and be valued on their ability to be fruitful.

An overemphasis on being can give rise to selfishness where our own satisfaction becomes more important than anything else. We become the centre of our own lives.

Understand who you are, be who you are

The point of discipleship is to reinforce your being through doing the right things.

Living as Jesus lived will draw out the true nature of who we are.

Studying the word of God will inform you of the truth of who you are. Be careful what you feed on!

Some say we should live from the overflow of the heart. But, the heart can be fickle;

> *Jer. 17:9 The heart is deceitful above all things…*

> *Prov. 4:23 Keep your heart with all vigilance, for from it flow the springs of life.*

The heart should not be disregarded, but should be held in a place of assessment so that we are not led astray by feelings. Guard your heart; enrich your life!

Key areas of development

So, what are we to do to maintain our development?

Worship

> *"People will always reflect something, whether it be God's character or some feature of the world. If people are committed to God, they will become like him; if they are committed to something other than God, they will become like that thing, always spiritually inanimate and empty like the lifeless and vain aspect of creation to which they have committed themselves."[16]*

Worship is about far more than singing songs, it is about a lifestyle that transforms.

Our corporate worship should embody the presence of God. As we meet together we should experience His presence in ways that will happen nowhere else. God loves to be at the centre of our meetings and make His presence felt. We should expect that, as we worship Him together, as a body, we will corporately reflect more of Him and His glory. Our corporate experience should be filled with the prophetic, encouragement, and empowering.

Our personal worship should serve to deepen our awe and understanding of God and the work of the Holy Spirit. It should also create a stronger foundation for personal growth and clarity in our sense of identity.

We must keep our worship pure. It must be all about Him. Any preferring of "idols" will pollute our relationship with God and undermine our inner self.

---

[16] Expositor's Bible Commentary

Psa. 115:4 "Their idols are silver and gold, the work of human hands. 5 They have mouths, but do not speak; eyes, but do not see. 6 They have ears, but do not hear; noses, but do not smell. 7 They have hands, but do not feel; feet, but do not walk; and they do not make a sound in their throat. 8 Those who make them become like them; so do all who trust in them."

If we turn to idols [pretty much anything that isn't the Living God], we ultimately become like them; be careful what you worship!

Renewal

Rom. 12:2 "Do not be conformed to this world, but be transformed by the renewal of your mind, that by testing you may discern what is the will of God, what is good and acceptable and perfect."

Feeding your mind with the right thing, alongside a consistent engagement with the Holy Spirit, will result in renewal.

A renewed mind thinks better! It carries a re-shaped thinking. A renewed mind hears and understands God better because it is more receptive.

Phil. 4:8 "Finally, brothers, whatever is true, whatever is honourable, whatever is just, whatever is pure, whatever is lovely, whatever is commendable, if there is any excellence, if there is anything worthy of praise, think about these things. 9 What you have learned and received and heard and seen in me—practice these things, and the God of peace will be with you."

If you are filling your head with good things, there is no room for bad!

You control your mind! You decide what gets in there and how it effects you. There is a discipline required here that we must develop.

I had a young pastor come to me once and, in the course of the conversation, he said to me, *"I don't get you, you enjoy action movies*". I asked why he thought that was a problem. He replied, *"Well, doesn't that make you a more violent person?"* I asked him what sort of movies he enjoyed. He told me *"Comedies"*. I replied, *"Well, it hasn't made you any funnier!"*

The point here is this; we have to be aware of what potentially changes our shape. I know, when I watch a movie, that its not real - its Hollywood! Therefore, I am not shaped by it and don't attempt to repeat the things I see. If something disturbs my inner peace I stop it immediately. These things can be different for each of us. Some things are bad for all of us, some things are good for all of us, but there is a whole mass in the middle where we need to make decisions based on who we are. Much like Paul's comments over meat offered to idols, if it offends you, don't do it![17]

If we fill our minds with the right things, do the right things, we will be filled with God's peace. We must protect that.

Discipleship

> *Matt. 28:16 Now the eleven disciples went to Galilee, to the mountain to which Jesus had directed them. 17 And when they saw him they worshiped him, but some doubted. 18 And Jesus came and said to them, "All authority in heaven and on earth has been given to me. 19 Go therefore and make disciples of all nations, baptising them in the name of the Father and of the Son and of the Holy Spirit, 20 teaching them to observe all that I have commanded you. And behold, I am with you always, to the end of the age."*

Jesus final instruction to His disciples was to make more disciples! Our challenge is to engage in this process of both being and making.

---

[17] 1Corinthians 8

Ongoing discipleship is God's plan for making us everything He created us to be! The intention is that we all learn to do the things that Jesus did and in the process become more like Him. More of this later.

Confidence

God is with us!

> *Rom. 8:31 What then shall we say to these things? If God is for us, who can be against us? 32 He who did not spare his own Son but gave him up for us all, how will he not also with him graciously give us all things?*
>
> *35 Who shall separate us from the love of Christ? Shall tribulation, or distress, or persecution, or famine, or nakedness, or danger, or sword? 36 As it is written, "For your sake we are being killed all the day long; we are regarded as sheep to be slaughtered." 37 No, in all these things we are more than conquerors through him who loved us. 38 For I am sure that neither death nor life, nor angels nor rulers, nor things present nor things to come, nor powers, 39 nor height nor depth, nor anything else in all creation, will be able to separate us from the love of God in Christ Jesus our Lord.*

Our confidence should be in the ever-present God who is for us! This inseparability should be our strength; God loves us and will never leave us alone.

We are more than conquerors!

God's presence and His provision fuel and sustain our purpose. If He is with us, we may experience set-backs but, ultimately, we win!

Individual, but not individualism!

A final thought here is that in our becoming, the objective is to find and become secure in our unique individuality. Not to indulge in individualism.

Individualism tends towards self-reliance and independence.

God wants us to celebrate our uniqueness and individuality whilst being thoroughly connected to fellowship in the church and being in fruitful relationships.

We should be individuals who are inter-dependent on each other and wholly dependent on God.

What now?

- Are you a worshipper?
  - Do you spend time worshipping...
    - In private?
    - At church?
- Are you allowing you mind to be renewed by regularly reading the scriptures?
- Are you engaging in the process of discipling others as well as being discipled yourself?
- Are you living with the confidence of knowing that God is with you?
- Are you rooted in fellowship with like minded Christians and allowing them to speak into your life?
- If you answered "no" to any of the above, its time for action!

Chapter 7: Continuing

Ruth E. Filmer

The Challenge

As Christians we are called to a higher level of living and being. We are called to know our identity in Christ and to live this out in the place he has called us to. We are surrounded by a culture that very often opposes the Kingdom culture that the Bible outlines for us. So some questions that need to be considered are, who or what do we allow to shape us?

Is it possible to be engaged with culture yet also be a follower of Jesus? Or is it very much a choice between one or the other?

How do we go on that journey of self-discovery, leaving behind our insecurities?

In Philippians 3.13-14 (NIV) Paul says, *'Forgetting what is behind and straining towards what is ahead, I press on towards the goal...'* Is it really that easy to forget the past and press on?

The Voice of Fear

In this age it is so important for us to know who we are and whose we are. It is so important that we know who God created us to be. When we have a deeper relationship with God, we gain an understanding of just how much God loves us and that perfect love drives out fear (1 John 4.18). Once we know how God sees us, once we know his love for us, we are no longer fearful of living how God intended and our behaviour will soon follow. This is the starting point.

In the appendix, I talk about Dr Leaf and her contribution to neuroscience. She describes a process we can go through to gradually kill off the unhealthy thoughts of fear and anxiety and grow a new healthy thought in its place. We have divine power from God to demolish strongholds and we can take our thoughts captive and bring them in line with what God says about us, instead of what the world says.

The way you use your mind brings change. It takes determination but it is possible to completely change your thought patterns, to actually change the physical structure of your brain, through using your mind effectively. You might have heard that it takes 63 days to form a habit, this is based on the same science. It takes 21 days to start to break down a negative thought and begin to grow a new one, another 21 days to establish the new thought and be rid of the old one and 21 days to solidify the new thought or habit, which totals 63 days. Obviously, this can vary slightly because if you have been believing the unhealthy thought for years and years, the process might take longer, but 63 days is the general pattern. It takes determination and a motivation to want to change, as the process can be very emotionally draining. You're basically doing brain surgery on your own brain!

We react to everyday life and process everything we experience dependent on our already developed habits or thoughts. The more we focus on one particular thought, the more it controls us. You have to choose to change your brain, choose to believe what God says about you. It is the mind that controls the brain and not the other way around. Our mind has to be fixed on what God says about us.

What's in a Name?

A couple of summers ago, we went to visit some friends and had a day trip into Wells. Apart from beautiful architecture, they also have a pretty cool playground. The main attraction is a wooden castle with ladders to climb, netting, slides and a very tall fireman's pole. The launching platform is about my eye level. My 7-year-old boy had been to many parks and had swung down many fireman's poles. He approached this one with caution, stood at the top of the platform, looked down, leant over the edge slightly and decided it was just a little too high for him, so he turned around and started climbing down the ladder. I shouted after him, "Hey! What is your name?"

"Caleb," he said, looking at me strangely as if he couldn't believe I had forgotten his name.

"And what does your name mean?" I asked.

"Brave" he said. There was a brief pause and then he caught my meaning. He climbed back up the ladder, went to the top of the fireman's pole, leant over the edge, took a deep breath and slid down the pole, absolutely elated with himself that he had made it to the bottom unharmed.

When you know who you are, who God says you are, it changes everything. It changes how you see yourself, which in turn changes how you behave. Psalm 100.3 (NIV) says, *'Know that the Lord is God. It is he who made us and we are his.'* When we pursue a relationship with God, it follows that we find out more about us and who we were created to be.

We are then free to be who we were created to be in a culture that demands we give up our beliefs to fear.

The Devil's Voice

While not wanting to give too much credit to the devil, I think it's important to acknowledge the voice of the devil within our culture. The devil is crafty and cunning and places seeds of doubt, which is apparent from his very first appearance in the garden with Adam and Eve. In Genesis 3.1, the serpent asks a simple question and a seed of doubt is sown. Did God actually say that you must not eat the fruit? Eve responds to say they can eat the fruit, just not from that specific tree or they will die. The serpent, having already gotten Eve to question herself, outright lies to her. 'You will not die! God just doesn't want you to have as much power as him. He doesn't want you to know as much as him. God is not thinking about your interests, only his own.'

We can learn so much from this about how the devil operates today. We can have this image of the devil as being loud and brash and shouty! But the devil can be very subtle and crafty in the way he operates. He deceives us and lies to us in ways that make sense to us and that play on our own wants and desires. He uses the culture around us to show us that it works for everyone else. He gets us to question God's love for us and other people's love for us. We fall and the devil disappears having done his work, leaving us with guilt and shame. He says things like, 'Did God really say no sex outside of marriage? Did God really say don't get drunk? Did God really say to put him first in everything? Did God really say he is your provider? Did God really say he would be with you through everything? Did God really speak that over your life? Did God really say he loves you?'

Once we allow doubt in, it is hard to think of anything else. It is so important to notice these subtle changes and thoughts and to catch them before they are allowed to grow and take hold. We need to practice that awareness and ensure we are living righteous lives, weighing everything up against the word of God.

The Voice of Apathy

Rob Peabody, author of 'Citizen: Your Role in the Alternative Kingdom'[18], suggests that there are two main things that hold us back from reaching all that we could in our relationship with God. These two things are apathy and fear. We have already talked a little about fear, but apathy can be just as lethal. Peabody says,

> 'Apathy continually tells us that we are OK... that we have done enough... Apathy allows us to try a few times to live this Kingdom life, but when results are not seen or frustration sets in, it tells us that it's not that big a deal and really isn't worth it. When people don't respond to our efforts or treat us poorly because of them, apathy lies us down and tells us it is no use.' P.184

Apathy, like the devil's voice, has a subtle but very harmful effect. We oftentimes don't even notice that it plays a part in our thinking, but it stops us from moving forward and breaking ground in our walk with God. Several times in the New Testament we are given a call to persevere and to not give up. Just being aware of our own apathy and reasons for not doing something, can cause us to challenge our behaviour and step up and persevere.

Our apathy and lack of motivation can come from either not being connected to God or not living out and serving God in what he has called us to. It is him that stirs up a passion in us and it is relationship with him that gives us

---

18 Peabody R. (2014), Citizen: Your Role in the Alternative Kingdom. Oxford: Lion Hudson plc

the motivation to carry on and fight his cause. It is God's gift to us to enjoy the work he has asked us and equipped us to do. God wants us to feel passionate about serving him and living out the purpose he has given us with enthusiasm and joy. If you are not passionate about your role within the Kingdom of God, I would suggest you are either serving in the wrong place or you have perhaps lost focus of your love for God. We are called to love and show honour to God in our serving and all that we do, so serving and using our gifts in this way shouldn't be a chore or a duty. It should be seen as a privilege and an honour to serve God using the gifts he has given us. We serve an incredible God who works everything together, giving each of us a unique part to play. If we can't see that, then perhaps we need to return to our first love.

Attitude is so important. What are the motives behind doing what you do? Do you come to God daily and serve out of your love for Him? Or is it a sense of duty to God or to the church? Is it out of love for a person or group of people? It is so important to love people of course, but that has to come out of an overflow of first loving God.

The Right Role

Being in the right place and the right role within God's Kingdom is also essential as it eases frustration and creates motivation to persevere even when results seem to be few. Our motivation comes from the act of serving rather than from the results we see or don't see. It is vital that we embark on a journey of discovering who we are and who we were made to be.

Earlier this year when it was my husband John's birthday, I took him out for breakfast. We went to a little family-owned café just down the road from where we live. Our next-door neighbours, a mother and son, both work there and were both there when we went in. We had a chat with them, and the mother started to recommend some of the cooked breakfast items off the menu and was telling us how excellent the food was there. Then she said, 'Well whatever you choose, I will be making it so it will be good!' We both had full English breakfasts with slight variations and the food was excellent! Our neighbour came out of the kitchen as we were leaving to ask how we had found the food and we said we had very much enjoyed it. She looked really pleased but also not at all surprised that we had enjoyed her food.

That there is someone who knows what she is good at and walks in it. She didn't come across as arrogant at all, but simply knew she was there to do a job and knew that she could do it well and she was passionate about it. Our neighbour is not British. We seem to have a British culture that is one extreme or the other. We either do ourselves down and say we're rubbish at everything and question if we've done a good enough job or the opposite, we puff ourselves up to be much bigger and better than we are!

When we discover the purpose and role that God has given us, we can speak out just as our neighbour did. We can say with confidence, this is what I've been put on this earth for, this is what I'm here to do and I can do it well. Our attitude needs to be one of knowing who we are and whose we are. Knowing that God has placed me here for a reason, with these gifts and abilities, with these passions and desires and then confidently working from that place.

We recently rolled out a SHAPE questionnaire throughout our church, a concept developed by Rick Warren. This asked people about their Spiritual gifts, Heart (passions and desires), Abilities, Personality and Experience. We have been meeting with individuals to talk through their answers to help them discover their purpose and area of serving that they are best suited to in order to try and eliminate frustration and see people serving with passion and purpose. If you are unsure of what you are called to, doing a spiritual gifts questionnaire can be a really helpful place to start, followed by getting feedback from those who know and love you.

Honour and Humility

Paul Gibbs is the leader of the global organisation 'Pais Movement' who create mission opportunities and gap years for young people. His teaching on Kingdom Culture is excellent and all gap year students go through this teaching and are encouraged to model kingdom culture in everything they do, as a lifestyle. In a chapter on 'Humbling and Exalting'[19], Gibbs disregards the dictionary definition of humility and says,

'True humility is to have a right understanding of who you are before God and men... Humility knows we are special, but only through the viewfinder of an awesome God.' P.225

It is clear from reading his work that Gibbs recognises we honour God by showing honour to self and others, and in order to do this we have to have a clear understanding of who we are before God but also before men. He unpacks a principle that says we don't do ourselves any favours by behaving as if we are insignificant but that we must show humility by honouring and serving others.

This is a far cry from our society that says each man for his own and whoever comes out on top wins! We need to think about our own circle of influence and how we can honour those in authority over us whilst also honouring those under our care. This calls for an awareness of knowing our place, knowing that we were called for serving others as part of our service to God.

---

[19] Gibbs P. (2011), The Cloud and the Line. Texas: Harris House Publishing

There is another important principle here, that when we work to serve others, we need to allow those people to have a voice into our lives. It gives us accountability but also helps us to grow and move forward as individuals. When we allow someone who is ahead of us in the journey to speak truth into us, it brings a new level of awareness and opportunity for growth. The ideal is having someone you trust, who puts God first and who shows care for you. Giving them permission to challenge you through the journey is a great way to move forward in becoming all God has called you to. Though of course this is a continual journey!

In the World, Not of It

As Christians we can find it hard to know where the line is in terms of engaging with the culture around us. We know that Jesus prayed for us to be in the world but not of it but putting this into practice is difficult. We can go from one extreme to the other by either getting in so deep we're not sure if we're still Christians or we remove ourselves completely from culture so that we are not engaged with it at all. When we are totally engaged with society and the culture around us there is no way for the people watching us to see that we are different and that we hold the truth of God in our lives. We may become 'Sunday Christians' whereby we go to church on Sunday but the rest of the week we watch inappropriate or ungodly content, we speak inappropriate or ungodly words and we behave in inappropriate and ungodly ways, meaning that anyone who knows we go to church becomes very confused about who we actually are and what it means to be a Christian. On the other hand, we can try to remove ourselves totally from culture and only engage with activities or content that is godly and holy. We then end up having only Christian friends and going only to Christian gatherings and are given no opportunity to show our faith to others at all. The middle ground seems difficult to find or even to define. How can I know who I am in God, know my true identity but also engage with culture that is so far removed from the kingdom of God?

In his brilliant book 'Plugged In'[20], Daniel Strange tackles this question head on and gives the tools to engage with culture whilst still being true to self. He believes it is absolutely necessary that we engage with culture. Jesus so often did and the way he did that was to turn the behaviours and beliefs of the culture completely on its head leaving people feeling challenged and questioning their beliefs in the way society do things. Strange uses a four-part process to do this: enter, explore, expose and evangelise. If we are to expose our culture for what it is then we first need to enter and explore that culture. He talks about sports as an example, in that sports people will often find their identity in their achievements to the point that it affects their moods and behaviours. If a person loses, they feel they have failed and that they are not good enough. If they win, they feel a sense of purpose and elation. If their sport was removed from them, who would they be? This is the part that needs to be communicated and exposed.

If I were a sportswoman (anyone who knows me is laughing at the thought...), I would enter that culture and engage with it but then would expose the culture for what it is by not allowing my mood or identity to be affected by my losses and wins. If I lose and still show contentment in myself and in who I know I am, that will speak volumes to the people around me and then gives me opportunity to evangelise, to give the reason why my identity is not grounded in sport but in Jesus. This same process can be followed with anything that culture engages with, whether it be a song, a film or any other form of activity or medium.

---

[20] Strange D. (2019), Plugged In: Connecting Your Faith with What You Watch, Read and Play. The Good Book Company

If we engage with culture, yet know who we are in God, we can see culture for what it is and call culture out on the way it thinks and behaves. We can engage with the people around us, people that we already have something in common with and who share similar interests, encouraging them to see how they are influenced by society and the hold that culture has on them. Then point them towards another way, where they can meet with their creator and the one who brings joy and contentment no matter what is happening around us. The important thing in all of this is that we are rooted and established in God's love and engaging with other people from that place.

A Final Word

If we are to pursue growth as a constant journey there are many things we can do, some of which have been outlined. We have to allow God to define us and ensure that what we believe about ourselves is in line with what God says about us. We do this by pursuing a relationship with him, spending time in the word and prayer. We must also allow others to speak into our lives and hear their feedback, again ensuring it lines up with what God says about us. We should be engaging with the culture around us but being true to self, whilst we do this. We are not made to live double lives, but to live lives that reflect the King and his Kingdom.

When we know God's truth about us, we can move forward and leave behind insecurities and fear. However, sometimes we need a bit of extra direction. Sometimes it isn't easy to forget the past and move forward. And sometimes we need a bit of help to grow in our own self-awareness to go beyond what our peers can offer us. There is absolutely no shame in asking for outside help in the form of counselling. This could be to deal with a past issue that won't be laid to rest, to gain a better understanding of yourself or to get support with a current issue that you are going through. If this is something that you feel you need, please do seek professional support. I recommend looking for someone who uses Person Centred therapy and who is registered with BACP (British Association of Counselling and Psychotherapy). I pray that you would have the strength and courage to face your demons head on and to walk in the truth of God's love for you.

Chapter 8: Maturity

Whilst the journey will take the rest of our lives, it is still possible to reach a place of maturity in our sense of identity which will provide some sense of well-being and fulfilment. This chapter seeks to encourage the journey and understand some things about the help we receive from the Holy Spirit.

> *Eph 4:11 And he gave the apostles, the prophets, the evangelists, the shepherds and teachers, 12 to equip the saints for the work of ministry, for building up the body of Christ, 13 until we all attain to the unity of the faith and of the knowledge of the Son of God, to mature manhood, to the measure of the stature of the fullness of Christ, 14 so that we may no longer be children, tossed to and fro by the waves and carried about by every wind of doctrine, by human cunning, by craftiness in deceitful schemes. 15 Rather, speaking the truth in love, we are to grow up in every way into him who is the head, into Christ, 16 from whom the whole body, joined and held together by every joint with which it is equipped, when each part is working properly, makes the body grow so that it builds itself up in love.*

If we are doing this right, what should the results look like? How can we measure progress? How will we know if its working?

We will know if we are becoming mature!

Maturity [teleios] means fully accomplished in Christian enlightenment, understanding and applying our faith. Then we are built up with an inner strength through revelation and encouragement.

The gift ministries [people] mentioned in this passage are super-disciplers! Their role is to bring us all to maturity in Christ. Central to that is our sense of self, our identity. So, how does Paul define maturity?

These are the attributes Paul sees, they are the hallmarks of a well developed sense of identity in Christ and the outworking of the discipleship and development strategy;

Unity of the faith

Living in fellowship, joined by mutual love, respect and doctrine, submitting to one another. This doesn't mean we agree on everything, it means we behave like grown-ups when we don't.

Knowledge of the Son of God

Growing intimacy with Jesus through worship, prayer and study. A personal responsibility which can be measured. We have an obligation to grow here.

The fulness of Christ

Living in the daily experience of fulness of life that can only come from relationship with Jesus. This is not just a feel-good thing but has practical out-workings.

No longer children

Childish thinking and behaviour becomes a thing of the past, maturing in relationship, open to correction and guidance, living like grown-ups.

No longer tossed to and fro

Not vulnerable to the schemes and manoeuvrings of this world and its culture, not jumping on to every new idea, being discerning in what you accept and who you follow.

Wise to the world

Not taken in by the culture, standards and values of this world that are anti-God.[21]

---

[21] For further discussion on culture see the appendix.

Speaking truth in love

Living in a place of openness and honesty with each other, saying what we mean, meaning what we say, doing and saying all things in love and acceptance.

Growing into Christ

We become more and more like Him in character, word and deed. This, again, should be observable and measurable.

Joined to the body

Totally immersed in the life of the church, fostering good relationships, living accountably, loving and encouraging others, being honest, open and vulnerable, finding your place and serving.

Working properly

Living out everything God has made you for, serving, ministering, reaching out.

Helping the body to grow

Contributing to the lives of others in such a way that they also grow and develop into everything God is calling them to be.

Building in love

> *1Cor. 13:13 "So now faith, hope, and love abide, these three; but the greatest of these is love."*

This looks like a tall order, but if we apply ourselves to the right things, with the Holy Spirit's help, they are attainable.

> *Heb. 12:1 Therefore, since we are surrounded by so great a cloud of witnesses, let us also lay aside every weight, and sin which clings so closely, and let us run with endurance the race that is set before us, 2 looking to Jesus, the founder and perfecter of our faith, who for the joy that was set before him endured the cross, despising the shame, and is seated at the right hand of the throne of God.*

Heaven is cheering us on!

Looking to Jesus as our example, let's run!

The role of the Holy Spirit

John 14:15 "If you love me, you will keep my commandments. 16 And I will ask the Father, and he will give you another Helper, to be with you forever, 17 even the Spirit of truth, whom the world cannot receive, because it neither sees him nor knows him. You know him, for he dwells with you and will be in you.

John 14:18 "I will not leave you as orphans; I will come to you. 19 Yet a little while and the world will see me no more, but you will see me. Because I live, you also will live. 20 In that day you will know that I am in my Father, and you in me, and I in you. 21 Whoever has my commandments and keeps them, he it is who loves me. And he who loves me will be loved by my Father, and I will love him and manifest myself to him."

What I love about these verses is that Jesus puts everything together in a succinct and strategic way!

In the intimacy of the last supper, He instructs His disciples on being and doing fuelled by the Holy Spirit.

Here is the process;

15 If you love me, you will keep my commandments.

Obedience comes first [doing]

It would be fair to say that the intention of obedience is often enough, that said, we must endeavour to be obedient. We have to give God something to work with!

16 And I will ask the Father, and he will give you another Helper, to be with you forever

The Holy Spirit is given in response, Jesus does not set us up to fail! If we are following Him, He will provide for us.

Another helper; just like Jesus!

With us forever.

You know him, for he dwells with you and will be in you

I will not leave you as orphans; I will come to you

Closer than a brother

Jesus sends the Holy Spirit as a replacement for Himself. He, as a man [through the incarnation], now sits on a throne in heaven [interceding for us]. He sends the Holy Spirit to do for us everything He would do if He was standing next to us.

He comes to guide, empower and release. He brings truth and wisdom.

You can't make it without Him.

Paul, through these verses has given us a template for success. A measure by which we can chart our progress. To be successful in developing our sense of identity we do need to keep a check on how we're doing, to review how things are going. As mature followers, secure in our identity, there should be no fear in this, only positive challenges to move us on.

Many people think that maturity is the same as longevity. *"I have been a Christian for 20 years so I must be mature"*. This is not a solid equation. Maturity in our life, faith, and our sense of identity, is measured by how much we have become like Jesus. He is the plumb line by which all of our life should be measured. Paul's list of attributes is a good starting place for us.

What now?

- Reflect further on the Bible verses in this chapter
  - How would you rate your level of maturity?
  - What are you going to do to improve?
- Are you learning to lean on the Holy Spirit?
- Are you allowing trusted friends to speak into your life?

Chapter 9: Making It Work

Failure to plan is a plan to fail. We need a plan, a road map, a sense of direction and an idea of what the destination should look like. This chapter, summarising much of this book, seeks to provide some tools for charting a path.

Putting together all of the principles of this book, our action plan should look something like this;

Cognisance

A journey towards understanding. If we don't understand the issues it will be hard to find solutions. Cognisance, in this context, has to do with self-awareness, identifying the issues and challenges, and understanding what we must do, on a personal level, to grow our sense of identity. We will undoubtedly need someone to help us with this, someone who knows us well, someone we trust.

The search for identity starts with understanding.

Value

We must understand that our personal value is found entirely in what God has to say about us. We were planned, designed, created for purpose and we are loved unconditionally. The world, culture and other people, will want to tell us different. Devalue us. Make us insecure and subdue us so that we submit to the culture and become a part of it. Understanding our value is our first line of defence and the solid foundation that we build on.

The search for identity requires that you know where your value lies.

Fellowship

The church is God's plan. It is His solution to the ills of the world. It is His nursery for growing mature Christians. It is home-base for developing our sense of identity. It is a necessity for survival and growth. Your wellbeing, maturing and sense of fulfilment is dependent on being firmly rooted in the fellowship of a local church. We have already recognised that all churches are not the same. So, find one that will encourage you, challenge you and support you. Then stay there!

The search for identity requires that you are rooted in fellowship.

Doing and being

It is important to understand the balance of doing and being. Doing [discipleship] is important for inner formation, that inner formation of our being then gives rise to a more natural and fruitful doing. Balance is important. Keeping the flow going is important.

The search for identity requires a balance of doing and being.

Journeying

Life is a journey. We must not try to live it all in 24 hours! The journey is filled with steps, some bigger than others. What we need is a sense of steady progress and not try to change everything over night.

It is likely we will not complete the journey in this life, but that's ok. Just keep stepping out and moving in the right direction.

The search for identity is a journey.

The maturity check

We need to continually be in a state of review. If we don't check where we are, and keep an eye on our direction, how will we know when we get there? It is good to get others involved in this process and have some objective views.

The search for identity requires ongoing assessment.

What will get us through this life with a genuine sense of achievement? What will enable us to feel fulfilled? What will make us fruitful and productive? What will make us secure in relationships? What will make us secure in our relationship with God?

The answer is simple, finding the real you and being secure in your identity.

Being the person God designed, created and calls you to be.

Identity growth check-list

☐ Make a start

☐ Set aside old misconceptions

☐ Prepare for growth

☐ Be sure you are established in a good church

☐ Open yourself to the work of the Holy Spirit

☐ Find a good mentor

☐ Engage with Biblical discipleship

☐ Instigate personal progress checks

☐ Keep moving, even after set-backs

☐ Review! [Go back to the beginning!]

Appendix: The Technical Bit

Ruth E. Filmer

What is Identity?

In a book all about identity and an appendix looking into the psychology of it all, it seems a good idea to see how the psychologists define identity. Erik Erikson[22] (1968) defines identity as a subjective feeling of sameness and continuity over time. It is a sense that you are being the same person in different places and different social situations. This person is recognised by others in terms of their attitudes and behaviour, as a continuity of character develops. Therefore, once identity is formed, it is reasonably predictable, and we can expect a person to behave the same way with the same reactions and character traits in different situations. My identity is the very core of who I am and everything flows from this.

So how do we find this core? How does it develop?

It is a bit of a stereotype of counselling and psychology that we must delve deep into the past to figure out what is going on in the present and while I would never want to dig deep into the depths of anyone's past, there is certainly something to be said for the early childhood years and the impact they have on future identity development.

---

[22] Erikson, E. (1968), Identity: Youth and Crisis. New York: W. W. Norton & Company

Attachment

Attachment theory, first described by John Bowlby[23] (1958 onwards), tells us that a sense of security is essential for the developing child to ensure they can create meaningful relationships throughout their lifetime and to thrive. The new baby forms a bond with the mother through 'attunement' or a constant connection through the mother understanding the wants and needs of the baby (Hughes, 1997[24]). The baby feels connected to the mother because the baby's emotional and physical needs are met. This creates a secure attachment and a secure base from which the baby can explore the world around him. This starts as young as birth (and some studies suggest from the womb). A baby's sight at birth is clear at 12 inches which is about the distance from the baby's face to the mother's face when feeding. This allows the baby to gaze at their mother and for the mother to respond. Then begins the journey of attunement whereby the baby matches the mother's facial expressions and starts to make sounds. The mother then responds with similar facial expressions and sounds. This whole process of a mother bonding with her baby encourages feelings of security and love in the baby and creates a secure platform for identity and self-esteem to grow.

As the baby grows older, the attachment to his or her caregiver grows stronger and the baby has a safe base from which to explore. This sense of safety and security gives the baby the freedom to explore their surroundings

---

[23] Bowlby, J. (1958) cited in Meins E. (2003) Emotional Development and Early Attachment Relationships in Slater, A. & Bremner, G. (2003) An Introduction to Developmental Psychology. Oxford: Blackwell Publishing

[24] Hughes, D.A. (1997), Facilitating Developmental Attachment: The Road to Emotional Recovery and Behavioral Change in Foster and Adopted Children. Maryland: Rowman & Littlefield Publishers, Inc.

knowing that their mother will be there if needed. If you watch a child that can walk or crawl and who has a little freedom, you will most likely see the child stay close to the mother whilst observing their surroundings, then they will explore close to their mother, then a little further away but will regularly return to their safe base, their mother. This process is essential to identity development as it is out of security and safety that we discover who we are.

Childhood and Adolescence

This journey continues throughout childhood with the child beginning to copy the behaviour of their caregiver. This is the next stage of identity development (Kroger 2007[25]) and it is where the child practices how to be a person in his or her own right. They will closely observe the people around them, especially those they are closest to. How often have you heard a parent say to a child, 'Do as I say, not as I do'? As parents, we would like our children to develop and grow far beyond our own growth but at this stage, the child only knows what he or she sees and copies this to practice their identity.

Adolescence is perhaps the stage of life where the most work is done in identity development as it is a shift from being reliant on the parent, looking to the parent for clues on how to behave and journeying into their own identity. This brings with it a lot of risk taking, experimentation and confusion as the teenager learns how to make their own decisions and live out being their own person in the big wide world. This is where the earlier years of attachment have a huge impact. If the attachment process is threatened, then the sense of security, belonging and sense of self is threatened too.

---

[25] Kroger, J. (2007), Identity Development: Adolescence through Adulthood. Second Edition. California: Sage Publications

Hughes describes this bond between mother and child as a 'central component of one's self, not simply an 'add-on' to be 'well-rounded' (Hughes, 1997, p.21). This sets the foundation for all future growth and development and can have huge implications for identity development. If a child has a good sense of security, they will engage in 'good' risk-taking behaviours, experimenting in ways that will have no lasting negative effect. They will have good levels of self-confidence and self-esteem. They will have a good idea of who they would like to be and who they are aiming to become and are quite likely to go a long way to fulfilling their potential. Adolescents, like all of us, are looking for acceptance. This acceptance can be gained through the risk of giving an honest opinion and gauging the reaction of others, to more negative risk-taking behaviours such as joining in with peers drinking too much.

Self-actualisation

Carl Rogers, widely known as the father of humanistic psychology, theorised about identity through his findings as a therapist. He believed that all people have a tendency towards becoming a better person and reaching their full potential. Rogers (1951) termed this 'self-actualisation' saying, "The organism has one basic tendency and striving – to actualise, maintain and enhance the experiencing organism" (p.487). Rogers meant that we have an innate motive towards being good people and reaching the highest potential possible for us. This is the main crux of identity formation and the goal is to become a 'fully-functioning person'. Rogers didn't see this as an end goal that people actually reach but more of a journey to becoming the best we can be and forever working to reach our potential. The end goal can only be reached if a person experiences a match between who they would like to be and who they actually are in terms of character, values, attitude and behaviour. To give an example, if I want to be a confident public-speaker, then I am fully functioning in this area when I can get up in front of people and speak confidently, believing that I have something to offer my audience. My self-worth is at such a level that I can do that confidently, without criticising myself or devaluing myself, yet still be looking for ways to better myself. This is just one area. To be a fully functioning person, you would feel this way across every area of your life!

When It All Goes Wrong

Despite having a theory whereby all people strive to become better, Rogers (1957) recognised that many people do not reach this goal, or even start this journey, as a result of external experiences. We have set-backs when we do not feel accepted or genuinely loved by the significant people around us and this impacts every area of our lives.

Years ago in my counselling practice I had ten sessions with a man in his twenties who was feeling out of control with his emotions. He was often troubled with scary thoughts that something terrible would happen at any moment, which gave him crippling anxiety attacks that he was struggling to cope with. He felt he couldn't talk to anyone about it and none of his friends or family knew he was coming for counselling. I worked with him on his fears and I believe it was a result of him feeling unloved and unaccepted in his family life and through childhood. He had a girlfriend and they were about to buy a house together, but he wasn't sure if she was truly in love with him. He felt jealous a lot of the time and was often questioning her and her motives. She didn't know he was coming for counselling either.

In my last session with him, after we had talked through a lot of his anxiety and the reasons behind it, he described how he had been feeling a lot better and that his irrational fears had become more manageable. I offered to do some couples counselling with him and his girlfriend and explained how I would take them through a process of getting to know each other better and being authentic with one another as a foundation for them to build their future on. He immediately declined my offer saying that he didn't think it would be a good idea to be that honest with his girlfriend! Even though he had done some good work and had begun to accept parts of himself, he was still far too unsure of himself to show anyone else who he really was and preferred to play a part as someone else in order to be loved and accepted. A recipe for disaster in my opinion!

This is an example of someone living out his day-to-day life and having a degree of 'normality' but not coming close to the potential of having a thriving relationship with his girlfriend. He didn't want to admit to her that he was struggling with anything or that he was weak, and he wasn't strong enough in his sense of self to be honest and open with the person he wanted to spend the rest of his life with. He was hiding his real identity from the people he loved the most.

Living in the Shadows

Carl Rogers termed this mismatch of outward presentation and inward feelings as 'incongruence'. In counselling training, a great deal of emphasis is placed on the student learning to be congruent within themselves. You cannot qualify as a counsellor unless you have developed this skill to some degree. Student counsellors have rigorous self-development training through small group sessions on the course and through their own one-to-one counselling sessions. They are also trained in picking up on and challenging incongruence in the client, which presents itself when the client says something, but it is clear that they feel another way. I'm sure we can all think of examples where a friend has said they were not bothered by someone's actions, but it is clear from their tone or body language that they actually feel very hurt. Or perhaps you know a person who presents as arrogant or talkative a lot of the time. This can often have a direct link to how insecure they feel on the inside. It is the role of the counsellor to pick up on these moments and challenge the person to consider and express their true feelings on the matter. Once expressed, it becomes easier to accept ourselves, the way we think, the way we are wired and to grow and change from that point.

Each of us is presented with a choice about whether we grow and develop ourselves to the point of congruence between our feelings and actions or whether we sink into the shadows, resulting in never really reaching the purposes of God for our lives. If we choose the former, it requires a constant journey of self-development which can only come through becoming more self-aware. We cannot work on areas of our lives that need attention if we do not know what those areas are! Self-awareness is the key to tackling self-development and growing into the true version of who we are, the version God intended us to be.

Neuroscience – another view

When I first began studying psychology over twenty years ago, I was taught that our brains were pre-disposed to certain things including genes. Every essay I wrote for my A-level ended with three options to explain any behaviour or mental state: a) nature,
b) nurture or c) the secret option where there is a dormant predisposition for it that is triggered by a life event. If you take the example of depression, the three

possible causes would be biology and genetic inheritance from parents who also suffer from a depressive illness, a traumatic life event such as a bereavement or a mixture of the two where a gene that you inherited is triggered by the traumatic life event. When doing my A-levels, secret option C was always the preferred option in any psychological study, which I found to be a cop out.

I'm so thankful for research and advances in science! We now know that a characteristic of the brain is neuroplasticity, which basically means that the brain can be moulded and changed. Our brains can be turned around and previous thoughts and memories can be reconstructed. I could never describe the science of this, so I've borrowed the description from Nicola Morgan[26], author of 'Blame my Brain'.

'The human brain contains about 100 billion nerve cells (neurons). Each neuron has a long tail-like part (axon) and many branches (dendrites – from the Greek word dendron, meaning tree). A neuron sends super-fast messages to other neurons by passing a tiny electrical current along its axon and across very tiny gaps (synapses) into the dendrites of other neurons. If the neurons did not communicate, your body would do nothing. Every single thing you do – every thought, action, sneeze, emotion, even things like going to the toilet – happens when the neurons send the right messages, very fast, through this incredibly complicated web of branches. Each time you repeat the same action, or thought, or recall the same memory, that particular web of connections is activated again. Each time that happens, the web of connections becomes stronger. And the stronger the connections, the better you are at a particular task. That's why practice makes perfect.'
P.11-12

---

[26] Morgan, N. (2013), Blame My Brain: The Amazing Teenage Brain Revealed. London: Walker Books

This works for self-esteem too. If we continually tell ourselves that we are worthless, not clever, ugly and so on, the connections in the brain are strengthening to a point where it becomes a central and core belief and everything we do comes out of that view. For example, adulthood depression might be caused by one childhood experience that led to a feeling of inadequacy, which has been re-emphasised in the brain by our own dwelling on the negative feeling and/or through a series of other experiences that confirmed and re-emphasised the feeling. We do in effect become self-fulfilling prophecies.

The good news is that recent studies on the brain say that this can be reversed thanks to the neuroplasticity of the brain (see the work of Dr Caroline Leaf)! This has massive implications for dealing with negative thinking and insecurities and developing self-worth. With enough education and effort, previous insecurities and negative thoughts that have defined us can be moulded and changed to become aligned with God's original plan and unique identity for each one of us.

I have recently discovered the Christian Neuroscientist Dr Caroline Leaf who adds to this saying our brains are originally wired for love and anything against love is a toxic thought we have allowed to implant, often without even realising it. There is something to be said for the power of words and especially bondage breaking scripture verses repeated daily. The desire for change is the key as with anything. Without the desire to change, we lack motivation to do anything. It requires hard work and patience to change brain structures!

Culture

So how does culture and society fit into this? What effect does our culture have on the development of our identity? Culture has a huge amount of influence, which could be a book in itself. We all have an inherent sense that we want to belong somewhere and often we look to the society we live in to find that sense of security and belonging, which means we then adapt to fit in. We want to be loved and accepted yet we live in a society that is becoming more and more lenient in its views compared to those of traditional Christianity. I have seen in my own experience younger Christians who want to fit in and therefore allow society to shape their identities but still want to follow God and are unsure about how the two match up. Invariably, as fallen humans, we go with the option that is most appealing.

In particular the rise of social media has had an impact on the development of identity in adolescents in general. This generation are perhaps given less opportunity to develop effective adult roles as much of their identity development takes place online, rather than in a face-to-face context. There is evidence to suggest that adolescent's self-esteem is directly affected by feedback on social media, seeing a higher self-esteem with more positive feedback and vice versa (Valkenburg, Peter & Schouten, 2006[27]). If use of social networking sites is the adolescents preferred way of engaging with peers, then this is cause for concern and will not be conducive to a sound sense of self-identity.

Furthermore, adolescents have access to peer relationships that parents may not wish their children to have. Teenagers are often more knowledgeable than their parents when accessing the internet, meaning that parents have little say in how the internet is used. This creates a whole world of identity experimentation where adolescents have the ability to

[27] Valkenburg, P., Peter, J. & Schouten, A. (2006), Friend Networking Sites and their Relationship to Adolescents' Well-Being and Social Self-Esteem, CyberPsychology & Behavior, Vol 9 (5). Mary Ann Liebert, Inc DOI: 10.1089/cpb.2006.9.584

create false online identities or experiment with different personas, gaining feedback from peers, some of whom they may not have met in a face-to-face context. More and more, adolescents are turning to a sense of belonging found in cyberspace, instead of in reality (Shifflet-Chila et al, 2016[28]).

Having an area of identity that can be experimented with in cyberspace is an alien concept to many adults but is the norm among this generation of adolescents. It gives teenagers endless opportunities to show themselves in different poses, situations and appearances to gain instant feedback from peers, which could be very liberating or could have detrimental effects. Rosen[29] (2012) suggests that we are increasingly using social media to put across opinions that we would not dare to share face-to-face and that the gap between real self and online self could grow larger and larger, creating a colossal incongruence between the 'real self' and the constructed self.

Responsibility of Construction

Each of us have had situations and circumstances that we have had to endure that we would rather not have gone through. However, each of us also has a choice about how much we let these experiences affect our day-to-day lives. We will, without a doubt, be shaped by these experiences but it is our responsibility to learn from the experience and turn a negative into a positive, rather than accepting and taking on board the negative. We each

[28] Shifflet-Chila, E., Harold, R., Fitton, V. & Ahmedani, B. (2016), Adolescent and Family Development: Autonomy and Identity in the Digital Age. Children and Youth Services Review 70, pp. 364-368

[29] Rosen, L. (2012), iDisorder: Understanding Our Obsession with Technology and Overcoming its Hold on Us, New York: Palgrave Macmillan

have a choice which determines the future of our identity construction and turning to faith in God during these times is by far the best way to find our true identity.

Useful Scriptures

Exodus 14.14

The Lord will fight for you, and you have only to be silent.

Exodus 15.2

The Lord is my strength and my song, and he has become my salvation; this is my God, and I will praise him, my father's God, and I will exalt him.

Joshua 1.9

Have I not commanded you? Be strong and courageous. Do not be frightened, and do not be dismayed, for the Lord your God is with you wherever you go.

Job 11.16-18

You will forget your misery; you will remember it as waters that have passed away. And your life will be brighter than the noonday; its darkness will be like the morning. And you will feel secure, because there is hope; you will look around and take your rest in security.

Psalm 16.8

I have set the Lord always before me; because he is at my right hand, I shall not be shaken.

Psalm 23.4

Even though I walk through the valley of the shadow of death, I will fear no evil, for you are with me; your rod and your staff, they comfort me.

Psalm 34.4

I sought the Lord, and he answered me and delivered me from all my fears.

Psalm 34.18

The Lord is near to the broken-hearted and saves the crushed in spirit.

Psalm 51.15

O Lord, open my lips, and my mouth will declare your praise.

Psalm 59.17

O my Strength, I will sing praises to you, for you, O God, are my fortress, the God who shows me steadfast love.

Psalm 86.13

For great is your steadfast love towards me; you have delivered my soul from the depths of Sheol.

Proverbs 3.5

Trust in the Lord with all your heart, and do not lean on your own understanding.

Isaiah 26.4

Trust in the Lord for ever, for the Lord God is an everlasting rock.

Isaiah 41.10

Fear not, for I am with you; be not dismayed, for I am your God; I will strengthen you, I will help you, I will uphold you with my righteous right hand.

Jeremiah 29.11

For I know the plans I have for you, declares the Lord, plans for welfare[a] and not for evil, to give you a future and a hope.

Zephaniah 3.17

The Lord your God is in your midst, a mighty one who will save; he will rejoice over you with gladness; he will quiet you by his love; he will exult over you with loud singing.

Matthew 6.33

But seek first the kingdom of God and his righteousness, and all these things will be added to you.

John 3.16-17

For God so loved the world, that he gave his only Son, that whoever believes in him should not perish but have eternal life. For God did not send his Son into the world to condemn the world, but in order that the world might be saved through him.

Romans 8.1-2

There is therefore now no condemnation for those who are in Christ Jesus. For the law of the Spirit of life has set you free in Christ Jesus from the law of sin and death.

Romans 8.32

He who did not spare his own Son but gave him up for us all, how will he not also with him graciously give us all things?

Romans 8.38-39

For I am sure that neither death nor life, nor angels nor rulers, nor things present nor things to come, nor powers, nor height nor depth, nor anything else in all creation, will be able to separate us from the love of God in Christ Jesus our Lord.

Romans 10.9

If you confess with your mouth that Jesus is Lord and believe in your heart that God raised him from the dead, you will be saved.

2 Corinthians 1.10

He delivered us from such a deadly peril, and he will deliver us. On him we have set our hope that he will deliver us again.

Ephesians 1 - the whole chapter!

Ephesians 6.13

Therefore take up the whole armour of God, that you may be able to withstand in the evil day, and having done all, to stand firm.

Philippians 4.6

Do not be anxious about anything, but in everything by prayer and supplication with thanksgiving let your requests be made known to God.

1 Thessalonians 5.16-18

Rejoice always, pray without ceasing, give thanks in all circumstances; for this is the will of God in Christ Jesus for you.

2 Timothy 1.7

God gave us a spirit not of fear but of power and love and self-control. (some versions say sound mind)

James 5.13

Is anyone among you suffering? Let him pray. Is anyone cheerful? Let him sing praise.

Revelation 21.4

He will wipe away every tear from their eyes, and death shall be no more, neither shall there be mourning, nor crying, nor pain any more, for the former things have passed away.

Further Reading

Identity Theft: Finding the Missing Person in You
© John Andrews, 2008
ISBN: 1905991118

Cleaning Up Your Mental Mess:
5 Simple, Scientifically Proven Steps to Reduce
Anxiety, Stress, and Toxic Thinking
© Dr Caroline Leaf, 2021
ISBN: 1540900401

The Purpose Driven Life:
What on Earth Am I Here For?
© Rick Warren, 2013
ISBN: 031033750X

Altar Ego: Becoming Who God Says You are
© Craig Groeschel, 2013
ISBN: 0310333717

A Long Obedience in the Same Direction:
Discipleship in an Instant Society
Eugene H. Peterson, 2021
ISBN: 0830848630

Other books by the same author

Culture, Context & Content, A Short Guide to Interpreting Your Bible
© David F Mansfield, 2009.
ISBN: 978-1-4452-4374-0

Getting Started, Leadership in the Local Church
© David F Mansfield, 2010.
ISBN: 978-1-4466-3972-6

**The Holy Spirit and the Church,
Reflections on 1 Corinthians 12, 13 & 14.**
© David F Mansfield, 2016
ISBN: 978-1-326-55493-4

All titles available on Amazon.

Printed in Great Britain
by Amazon